PHILIPPIANS
the Joyful Woman

6-WEEK BIBLE STUDY

BY LISA THOMPSON

Philippians: *The Joyful Woman*

Self-Published by Faith Journey Bible Studies
Revised Edition © 2016 Lisa Thompson
Original Copyright © 2014 Lisa Thompson
Cover Design © by Dave Eaton Creative

ISBN: 1530221250
ISBN-13: 978-1530221257

Printed in the United States of America

http://www.faithjourneybiblestudies.com

Philippians: The Joyful Woman

Table of Contents

About Faith Journey Bible Studies

In 2003 I took the biggest risk thus far in my faith and invited eighteen women in my neighborhood to a home for their first ever Bible study. I wasn't in the greatest spiritual shape myself and wasn't certain I knew the Bible well enough to lead the study. However, I was sure that I had tasted the sweetness of God's Word in my own life and that my faith journey was worth sharing with others.

Over the past several years the group has grown into many groups bringing women of all faith backgrounds and maturity levels together each week to study God's Word, build deeper relationships, and hold each other accountable as we grow in our faith in God together. There is something very unique about meeting in a home and sharing each other's faith journey with women you "do life" with. These are the women you run into at your kids' schools and activities, the gym, coffee shop, grocery store, or when walking in your neighborhood.

Because Faith Journey Bible Studies are inter-denominational and attract women in all places of life, women come! For some women it is much easier to walk into a home than to go into a church for Bible study. Also, Faith Journey Bible Studies have drawn women who may not be connected to a church or who may have minimal commitments at their church. As women begin to see the power of God's Word working in their lives and the lives of those around them, their desire to make Christ part of their daily life grows deeper. I have seen many women begin going to church, go back to church, or get their kids and husbands involved in church. They taste and see that the Lord is good and yearn for more!

In many ways Faith Journey Bible Studies have become bridges between the various churches and families in our community. Currently in my group there are over fifteen churches represented. What a beautiful picture of church unity and the Body of Christ!

Over time God began to grow within me the desire to have more women connected to a group like mine. Having four kids gives you incredible access into people's lives. While sitting on the sidelines at all the football, swim, soccer, and basketball games, I hear stories about failing marriages, health concerns, parenting challenges, job and financial troubles, and identity and self-esteem issues. I listen to these stories and in the back of my mind I think, "I would love for her to come to our Bible study," or "What a great support this would be," or, "If she only knew God's Word, it would change her whole perspective on how she sees her circumstances and give her hope."

God also gave me the burden to encourage friends in my life who are mature in their faith and have a heart for women in their neighborhoods to begin studies as well. For the past several years I have had the privilege of meeting monthly with women who stepped out and answered the call. It is a real encouragement to me to hear not only how God is working in their groups, but also how God is working in their own personal faith journeys. I have had much to learn through leading this Bible study and I am so thankful for the ways God has grown my faith and given me His heart to encourage others to step out of their Christian comfort zone and let Him transform their lives in new and exciting ways.

The theme of this study is *The Joyful Woman*. Paul wrote this letter to the Philippian church from prison where he was chained day and night to a Roman soldier and was suffering and facing a possible death sentence. Yet, he wrote with confidence, strength, and joy! The believers in Philippi experienced much of the same life issues we deal with today, and this letter is filled with guidance for us on everyday living. There is no doubt Paul knew the secret to living joyfully despite difficulties we may face or chains that may bind us and he makes it clear that no matter what each day brings, we can, with Christ's power, live victoriously and joyfully despite our circumstances. As you go through this study, my prayer for you is that you will learn how to experience the kind of joyful strength that Paul had.

I thank God that He has given me another opportunity to provide a resource designed to encourage and draw each of you into His Word. My prayer is that this study will help illuminate the Truth, give you greater confidence in reading your Bible, and help you discover all that God wants to tell you through His Word by the power of His Holy Spirit. I also pray that every time you open your Bible, you will receive encouragement from God, grow in your faith by being rooted in His Word, and bear much fruit that is pleasing to Him as you learn to abide in Jesus!

Blessings,

Blessed is the man who trusts in the LORD, whose confidence is in Him. He will be like a tree planted by the water, that sends out its roots by the stream. It does not fear when heat comes; its leaves are always green. It has no worries in a year of drought, and never fails to bear fruit.
Jeremiah 17:7-8 (NIV)

Welcome to Faith Journey

Welcome women! This will be an exciting year of growing, learning, and sharing God's Word together. Below are some suggestions that will make Faith Journey a place of encouragement for you.

Come as often as you can....

God is going to be teaching you some exciting things about His relationship with you through your study in the book of Philippians. Try to spend time reading the Bible passages, answering the study questions, and praying that the Holy Spirit will reveal God's truth to you. Some weeks the unexpected happens and you may not get your study done. Please come anyway! This is your group, and you will be greatly encouraged by the interaction and sharing among the women even if you didn't get your study done. Also, feel free to pop in late or leave early if you need to. *He is like a tree planted by streams of water that yields its fruit in its season, and its leaf does not wither. In all that he does, he prospers (Psalm 1:3, ESV).*

Come as you are...

There may be rough weeks in your life where Faith Journey is the last place you feel like going. Part of what makes us feel loved and accepted within a group is to know that the other members of the group are not judging us. It is therefore important that everyone refrain from judging others and instead look inward at the growth God is doing in their own lives rather than on what He needs to do in someone else's life! *You, therefore have no excuse, you who pass judgment on someone else, for at whatever point you judge another, you are condemning yourself, because you who pass judgment do the same things (Romans 2:1, NIV).*

Come to a safe environment...

It is important to create an environment that is safe and comfortable for personal sharing. This means that when someone in your group expresses personal issues, they are trusting that you will not share this information outside of the group. Confidentiality is absolutely necessary in order for women to feel safe and be able to share their hurts as well as their joys. It is also important that you consider limiting your sharing to your own personal needs rather than the needs of others. *Do not go about spreading slander among your people. Do not do anything that endangers your neighbor's life. I am the Lord (Leviticus 19:16, NIV).*

Come for support…

Take time during the week to share prayer requests and pray for one another, and in so doing, you will know how best to care for one another's needs. A phone call, hand written note, coffee chat, or hike together are some great ways of building friendships within your group. *"A new command I give you: Love one another. As I have loved you, so you must love one another. By this all men will know you are my disciples, if you love one another"* (John 13:34-35, NIV).

Come for variety…

Variety is the spice of life! A Faith Journey group is made up of women who come from varied church backgrounds or none at all. This group is not about which church one may or may not attend, but about individual journeys with God. *But, "Let the one who boasts boast in the Lord. "For it is not the one who commends himself who is approved, but the one whom the Lord commends.* (2 Corinthians 10:17-18, NIV).

Common Obstacles Encountered in a Faith Journey Group

By God's grace, your experience in Faith Journey this year will produce incredible spiritual **growth** in your life. However, be aware of potential **obstacles** that may pop up each week threatening to keep you from going to Bible study. The following obstacles are just a few of the ones you may encounter with some suggestions for overcoming them.

Going forward...

Poor decisions we made yesterday can impede our growth from happening today. You can't change the past but you can change your future. As you approach God and confess your mistakes and sins to Him, He washes your guilty conscience and calls you innocent. Learn to look at your mistakes as areas God wants to grow your faith and free you from unnecessary baggage you may carry. Your weekly time in Faith Journey is designed to help you take hold of the ways God has purposed for YOU today and tomorrow. *Forgetting what is behind and straining toward what is ahead, I press on toward the goal to win the prize for which God has called me heavenward in Christ Jesus (Philippians 3:13b-14, NIV).*

Repentance...

Your sins may prevent you from coming each week. Guilt, regret, and defeat are symptoms of sin that have not been put before the throne of Grace. As you confess your sins to God, He will free you of the ways you condemn yourself, but He also desires that you ask Him for help so that you can become less and less of a repeat offender. Know that when you are at your Faith Journey group, you are sitting among other sinners and you are not alone in your struggles. *Therefore confess your sins to each other and pray for each other so that you may be healed (James 5:16a, NIV). Repent, then, and turn to God, so that your sins may be wiped out, that times of refreshing may come from the Lord (Acts 3:19, NIV).*

Other people's issues versus my issues...

One of the biggest challenges for women when they are in a group setting is other women. Bible studies attract needy and imperfect people. Faith Journey creates a place where women feel the freedom to be authentic and real. Women are prone to keep things together on the outside but being in God's Word does not allow us to hide in that way. The result is that we see the flaws and imperfections of others. Don't miss out on your own growth because you are so busy making sure growth is happening for everyone else. Learn to extend the same grace that God extends to you every day. We are all works in progress and one day when we enter heaven we will be in awe of God's completed work in each one of us. *For in the same way you judge others, you will be judged, and with the measure you use, it will be measured to you (Matthew 7:2, NIV). Accept one another, then, just as Christ accepted you, in order to bring praise to God (Romans 15:7, NIV).*

Weakness...

There are some weeks when we are tired and overwhelmed by life. When you experience physical symptoms of stress and fatigue, it may be a sign that you are relying too much on your own strength rather than relying on God's strength to get you through your day. Think of Faith Journey as your pit stop in the middle of the week where you can fuel up. You will also be reminded that the fuel you need to be running on is Jesus Supreme! *I can do all things through Him who strengthens me (Philippians 4:13, ESV). My grace is sufficient for you, for my power is made perfect in weakness (2 Corinthians 12:8, NIV).*

Time...

Many women are super involved in several areas of responsibility and often have multiple competing demands for their time which can take precedence over getting their study done. When you are feeling overwhelmed with life, ask God to help you make Him your priority and trust Him that He will help you get those other important things done. God is so pleased by the sacrifices we make to pursue our relationship with Him and the spiritual growth He desires for us. *Like newborn babies, crave pure spiritual milk, so that by it you may grow up in your salvation, now that you have tasted that the Lord is good (1 Peter 2:2-3, NIV).*

Hardships...

There will be times this year when some of you may go through very difficult circumstances. Our nature is to pull away from others and go into a cave or place of hiding. We assume that we are left alone to struggle with things like marriage problems, financial pressures, chronic pain, depression, or overwhelming parenting challenges. However, the support you need may come from your Faith Journey group. Don't worry if your study is not done or you are not in a good place emotionally. Just come as you are. Retreat in the back of the room and fill up on God's Word and encouragement from the other women. You may be surprised to see how many others are experiencing similar hardships! *We can rejoice, too, when we run into problems and trials, for we know that they help us develop endurance (Romans 5:3, NLT). We pray... so that you may live a life worthy of the Lord and please him in every way: bearing fruit in every good work, growing in the knowledge of God (Colossians 1:10, NIV).*

Study Format

This study guide was written keeping in mind that we all learn and retain information differently. We also experience God differently. Each section provides different ways to connect with God and ways to practice some of the different spiritual disciplines He has provided for us to welcome Him into the busy and chaotic places of our lives. It takes time to find your groove and discover the ways you best interact with God through His Word. This Bible study resource will help guide you through the weekly passages. There is no right or wrong way to complete the lessons. You have the freedom to skip questions or even whole sections – and yes, leaving blanks in your study is okay.

Is This Your First Ever Bible Study?

If you consider yourself a seeker and this is your first ever Bible study, welcome! I thought of you so much as I wrote this. I've thought about the faith questions you might have. I've wondered about what might stand in your way of having a relationship with Jesus Christ. And I've wondered why you may have said yes to come to Bible study in the first place.

As you go through the study, be an observer. Accept that you may not be able to answer all of the questions, and that many things may not make sense to you right now. That is okay. You have the incredible opportunity to learn from other women in your group what having a personal relationship with Jesus looks like. And, you will quickly realize that you have much in common with these women. They are imperfect with lots of struggles just like you, they don't understand the Bible entirely, and they too have questions regarding their Christian faith. However, by faith, they have made a decision to trust God and His Word and walk differently than the rest of the world.
Each of our faith journeys begin at the Cross by recognizing the incredible love and sacrifice God provided through His son, Jesus Christ, so that we could be in a personal and intimate relationship with Him. There is nothing we did to deserve this gift and nothing we can do to earn this gift except surrender our lives to Jesus.

Are You Fairly New to Bible Studies?

If you are fairly new to studying the Bible, do not become disheartened when you read the passage and nothing makes sense. Ask the Holy Spirit to be your guide and show you what He wants you to learn. Observe how the other women are interpreting and pulling out truths from the passage, and remember to ask questions. I have had some really smart women in my group who excelled in college and in the workplace feel really ignorant when they approached studying the Bible. Keep in mind, the Bible was written to change hearts, and it is important that you don't just study the Bible to gain knowledge but that you also allow God's Word to penetrate your heart.

Are You a Seasoned Veteran of Bible Study?

If you have been studying the Bible for a while, try to dig beyond what you already know. Explore new truths and ways God wants to continue teaching and revealing Himself to you. It is very easy in our maturity to lose the spark and forget the basics of our Christian faith. One of the reasons why I love being in a group with so many young believers is that it ignites my own fire that can become dim over years of walking with the Lord. In many ways, it is the same reason I love being around a newly married couple. The newness and freshness of their relationship is contagious. May this study refresh and ignite those places in your heart that God wants to speak to.

The Real Goal of Bible Study...

Finally, women are guilty creatures. The level of guilt women feel when they don't get their Bible study done or skip out on going to their group amazes me. Maybe you are prone to feeling that studying the Bible is just another task to get done on your already busy schedule. Keep in mind that the goal of Bible study is to spend time with God, to learn about Him, and discover who you are in the eyes of the One who created your innermost being. It is very personal and each one of us experience God differently.

God is pursuing you every day, inviting you to say, "I am available." God does not give guilt trips. However, the enemy does, and he will use guilt to try to keep you from going to your study. Pay attention to those feelings if you are having one of those hectic weeks. My encouragement to you is to create time each day, as little or as much as you can, to connect with God through the weekly passage and this study resource. When life brings you the unexpected and you can't complete your study, go to your group anyway and learn from others. You will be renewed in your faith and may find yourself motivated to get your study done the following week so that you don't miss out!

Don't worry if you don't complete every section or question in each lesson. Leaving blanks is okay! There are a lot of different ways to interact with God and His Word. You will discover what works best for you and how you break up the lesson each week!

How to Use This Study

Each lesson follows the same F.A.I.T.H. format and moves through the inductive Bible study principles of observation, interpretation, and application.

$\mathcal{F}$ *Focus on the Passage*

$\mathcal{A}$ *Admit Where You Are*

$\mathcal{I}$ *Interpret the Passage*

$\mathcal{T}$ *Take the Passage into Your Life*

$\mathcal{H}$ *Hear From God*

$\mathcal{F}$ **Focus on the Passage**

The Word of God is like a mirror. When we approach it, there are incredible things that we will see about the character of God and also about our own character. Even though these stories, teachings, parables, and letters were written over 2000 years ago, they remain applicable today! Begin to see God's Word as a way to interact with Him and make the connections with what is going on in your life that week. God wants us to respond to His written Word. He wants to hear our appreciation, our humility, our fears, our confusions, our anger, our hopelessness, and our questions.

Focus on the Passage questions will help guide you as you study your weekly lessons. Use the margins to respond to the questions. The English Standard Version (ESV) Bible translation was used for the majority of weekly passages in this study. Individual verses from the New American Standard Bible (NASB), New International Version (NIV), New King James Version (NKJV), and New Living Translation (NLT) have been quoted as well. You can find different Bible translations as well as a variety of Bible commentaries at www.biblegateway.com or www.blueletterbible.org.

Questions to ask yourself as you read a Bible passage:

1. What is going on in the passage? *(Who, What, Where, When, Why, and How)*

2. What are the repeated words or contrasts?

3. What are the natural divisions in the passage?

4. What is the theme?

5. What questions do you have?

6. What word(s) bring you comfort?

7. What truth(s) are you having a hard time accepting?

8. What are you thankful for?

A   *Admit Where You Are*

Each weekly lesson asks questions that will help you discover your current way of thinking, spiritual understanding, and life circumstances. *Admit Where You Are* questions will help you connect your own life circumstances to the spiritual truths revealed in the passage. This allows you to be raw and honest before God. Establishing your baseline of current thinking makes it possible for you to look back later and see how the Word of God has transformed you. You will be amazed!

I   *Interpret the Passage*

Historical Context – Look up names, places, historical events, and cultural facts.

Cross Referencing – One of the ways we can begin to interpret a passage we are reading is by looking at other parts of Scripture that address the same theme or topic to gather additional insight and understanding.

Definitions – Use a dictionary, Bible dictionary, or concordance, to define words you want to know more about or are unsure of.

Commentaries – Bible commentators have been cited throughout the study to help enrich your understanding of a passage.

Hebrew/Greek – The Bible was originally written in Hebrew and Greek. Knowing the origin of a word can be helpful in understanding its meaning.

Bible Translations – Reading Scripture from different versions of the Bible, can also help shed light on the meaning of a passage.

T   *Take This Passage into Your Life*

The questions vary week to week, but they all focus on:

1. What you have discovered about God and His character and about yourself and your need for Him.

2. What specific situation, relationship, or circumstance in your life the passage addressed.

3. What unbelief, wrong attitude, or rebellious behavior in your life was revealed.

4. What action you need to take to apply God's truth to your life.

𝓗   *Hear from God*

Often when we finish up our Bible study we feel we are done. We have answered the questions and completed all the sections. However, during our quiet moments with God as we are studying and responding to our weekly passages, God wants to speak to our hearts and change us from the inside out. We won't hear from Him if we don't take time to listen to what He has to say. Sometimes our time with God is a one-way, or a my-way, conversation. God wants it to be a two-way conversation, and the *Hear from God* questions will give you an opportunity to hear and discern His voice through Scripture. I encourage you to get a notebook or journal and write down the things God is teaching you from this study in the book of Philippians.

Journey Challenge

Each lesson you will be encouraged to let God's word "dwell in your hearts" by memorizing a verse from the passage being studied. If you practice memorizing this verse a few times a day, you'll have it memorized by the time you meet with your Faith Journey group!

Feel a Bit Lost When it Comes to Bible Study? Have No Fear!

Have you ever been in a situation where your pastor or Bible study leader asks you to open your Bible to some unfamiliar book like Obadiah? Quickly, you see people all around you flipping through the pages of their Bibles appearing to know exactly where they are going. It can be stressful when you don't know where to turn. I finally took the time to understand how the Bible was put together and the purpose for each book. I also got Bible tabs, which I recommend. My point is, don't wait to discover the beauty and order of such an amazing book. Start today!

For many years when it came to reading the Bible, I usually read from the New Testament. I found it easier to understand and loved the applications I could use in my everyday life. I rarely found myself in the Old Testament, except when reading *Proverbs* or the *Psalms*. I had a hard time understanding how stories in the Old Testament written over 2000 years ago could relate to me today. There are so many rules, wars, crazy sins and characters to follow, and God seemed angry and distant.

The problem was that the Bible was not written for spectators but for participators. I had been reading much of the Bible as a spectator, at times judging the actions of Israel or key characters in the Bible. "How could Abraham lie to Pharaoh and tell him his wife was his sister?" Or, "I can't believe Israel continued to complain and be bitter towards God after all He had done for them." Or, "I can't believe Eve bit the apple when God gave her everything in the Garden of Eden. What's up with that?" When you read the Old Testament as history, for example, that was back then and this is now, then you miss the whole point as to why God inspired so many authors to write the Old Testament. He has something very important to tell us, and He used a small group of people, Israel, to reveal Himself to us and to reveal how hopeless and sinful we are apart from Him.

All the pieces of the puzzle finally came together that showed me what the Bible is all about. The Bible is the greatest love story ever told, and each book of the Bible reveals in different ways, how significant we are to God and the plan He had from the very beginning that would enable us be in a restored relationship with Him. The following pages are a quick summary of every book in both the Old and New Testaments. You will see themes, patterns, order, and spiritual truths. Begin reading the Bible as a story. There is a setting, characters, plot, climax, and conclusion. As you learn to identify each part of the Biblical story, you will gain a clearer understanding of how you fit into it.

For those of you who are new to Bible study, I have put together some brief notes on the Bible, the benefits of studying the Bible, and how to get started with your study in the book of Philippians.

Recommendations for Reading and Studying the Bible

All Scripture is God-breathed and is useful for teaching, rebuking, correcting and training in righteousness, so that the man of God may be thoroughly equipped for every good work.
2 Timothy 3:16 (NIV)

As you approach Scripture...

- Clear away any distractions: TV, kids, laundry basket, phones, Facebook, e-mails, texting, work tasks, and hunger.
- When you open your Bible, ask God to open your mind and heart to receive His truth and the Holy Spirit to be your guide.
- The Bible is our primary source, and the Holy Spirit is our primary teacher. John reminds us that the Spirit abides in us in order that we might be enabled to distinguish truth from error.
- John teaches that the Spirit of God, living in each believer, is our personal, private tutor. To be sure, God has given us human pastors and teachers for our edification *(1 Corinthians 12:28)*, but remember that they are in addition to and not a substitute for the Holy Spirit. And so, the humblest believer in Christ may be taught of God through His Word, even when human teachers are not available. *As for you, the anointing which you received from Him abides in you, and you have no need for anyone to teach you; but as His anointing teaches you about all things, and is true and is not a lie, and just as it has taught you, you abide in Him (1 John 2:27, NASB).*

What if you don't get it...

Just because you pray for guidance and study hard doesn't mean you are going to understand everything in the Bible. Since the Bible is God's Word, and because there are things that He has kept a mystery, it is inevitable that we will not be able to fully understand every Scripture. *The secret things belong to the Lord our God, but the things revealed belong to us and to our children forever, that we may follow all the words of this law (Deuteronomy 29:29, NIV).*

- **Rather than focusing on the things we don't know, we need to cherish and obey the things God has revealed to us.** With God's Word as your map and His Spirit as your compass, you're sure to stay on course.

- **Be patient.** God may choose to reveal something read in Scripture that morning or later that week. Your group discussions through Bible study will also give insight. Try to remember that God's view of time is different than our view of it.

- **This is a process.** God is most pleased by our obedience to read and grow in His Word. He promises to make Himself known through Scripture. Because the Bible is God's "living word," God will continue to teach you things over the years, even from passages you have studied before.

The Lord is with you when you are with Him. If you seek Him, He will be found by you, but if you forsake Him, He will forsake you (2 Chronicles 15:2b, NIV).

But from there you will seek the LORD your God and you will find him, if you search after him with all your heart and with all your soul (Deuteronomy 4:29, ESV).

Just like the most precious gemstones that can be found by searching for them and digging them out of the ground with great effort, we too must search for and dig out the most precious treasures of God's wisdom in His Word!

Personal Benefits of Reading and Studying the Bible

The Bible promises...

Comfort, strength, hope, wisdom, joy, purpose, power, and a transformed life! *But grow in the grace and knowledge of our Lord and Savior Jesus Christ. To Him be the glory both now and forever! Amen (2 Peter 3:18, NIV).*

Knowing God's Word...

Helps us to know who God is. *And that from childhood you have known the sacred writings which were able to give you the wisdom that leads to salvation through faith which is in Jesus Christ (2 Timothy 3:15, NASB).*

Helps us resist temptation. *I have hidden your word in my heart that I might not sin against you (Psalm 119:11, NIV).*

Helps us experience His power to change. *And do not be conformed to this world, be transformed by the renewing of your mind, so that you may prove what the will of God is, that which is good and acceptable and perfect (Romans 12:2, NASB).*

Helps us discover His direction for our lives. *Your word is a lamp to my feet and a light for my path (Psalm 119:105, NASB).*

Helps us share our faith. *Always be prepared to give an answer to everyone who asks you to give the reason for the hope that you have (1 Peter 3:15b, NIV).*

Helps us recognize counterfeit religions. *Now these were more noble-minded than those in Thessalonica, for they received the Word with great eagerness, examining the Scriptures daily to see whether these things were so (Acts 17:11, ESV). Do your best to present yourself to God as one approved, a workman who does not need to be ashamed and who correctly handles the word of truth (2 Timothy 2:15, NASB).*

Helps us discern right from wrong. *All Scripture is inspired by God and profitable for teaching, for reproof, for correction, for training in righteousness; so that the man of God may be adequate, equipped for every good work (2 Timothy 3:16-17, NASB).*

Specific benefits for your life...

There are some additional benefits we reap every day by being in God's Word. Read through the list below and check those personal benefits you hope to experience more of throughout your study in the book of Philippians. Look up the verses and underline them in your Bibles with the date.

- God's Word brings true health, fruitfulness, prosperity and success in everything we do. *(Psalm 1:3)*

- The Word of God has healing power; it has the power to deliver us from oppression. *(Psalm 107:20, Matthew 8:8, Matthew 8:16)*

- God's Word is cleansing. If we act according to God's Word, our way will be cleansed. *(Psalm 119:9, John 15:3, Ephesians 5:26)*

- The Word of God, hidden in our hearts, keeps us from sin. *(Psalm 119:11)*

- God's Word is our counselor. As we delight in God's Word, it becomes a rich source of counsel and guidance for us. *(Psalm 119:24)*

- God's Word is a source of strength. *(Psalm 119:28)*

- God's Word is a source of life. *(Psalm 119:93, Matthew 4:4)*

- God's Word is a source of light providing wisdom and guidance. *(Psalm 119:105, Psalm 119:130)*

- God's Word gives peace to those who love it; they are secure, standing in a safe place. *(Psalm 119:165)*

- When the Word of God is heard and understood, it bears fruit. *(Matthew 13:23)*

- God's Word has inherent power and authority against demonic powers. *(Luke 4:36)*

- Jesus Himself – His eternal person – is described as the Word. When we are into the Word of God, we are into Jesus. *(John 1:1)*

- Hearing God's Word is essential to eternal life; you cannot pass from death into life unless you have heard the Word of God and received it. *(John 5:24, James 1:21, 1 Peter 1:23)*

- Abiding or living in God's Word is evidence of true discipleship. *(John 8:31)*

- God's Word is the means to developing godly character. *(John 17:17)*

- God can do dramatic works through the Holy Spirit as His Word is being preached. *(Acts 10:44)*

- Hearing God's Word builds our faith. *(Romans 10:17)*

- Holding fast to the Word of God gives us assurance of our salvation. *(1 Corinthians 15:2)*

- The faithful handling of the Word of God gives the ministers of the Word a clear conscience for they know that they have done all they can before God. *(2 Corinthians 4:2, Philippians 2:16)*

- The Word of God is our sword of the Spirit, our equipment for spiritual battle, our offensive weapon. *(Ephesians 6:17)*

- The Word of God works effectively in those who believe. *(1 Thessalonians 2:13)*

- The Word of God is not dead; it is living and active and sharper than any two edged sword. The Word of God can probe us like a surgeon's expert scalpel, cutting away what needs to be cut out and keeping what needs to be kept. *(Hebrews 4:12)*

- The Word of God is our source of growth. *(1 Peter 2:2, 1 Corinthians 2:1-5)*

Even though the Old Testament was written over 2000 thousand years ago, this is your story as well! It's the story of your sin, your disobedience, your need, and the Savior that came down to reveal Himself to you. It is a timeless story of humanity's need to be redeemed, and within the history of Israel, you'll discover who you really are and who you can become when you trust your life to Christ!

Summary of the Bible

The Bible...

- The Bible is God's Word written over a period of about 1,600 years by more than 40 different human authors writing under the guidance of the Holy Spirit. (*2 Peter 1:20-21*)

- The word Bible comes from the Greek βιβλια — biblia, meaning "books".

- There are two parts - Old Testament (39 books) and New Testament (27 books).

- Testament means covenant or arrangement between two parties.

- God gave the Old Covenant to Moses for the people of Israel. (*Exodus 24*)

- Later, God announced through the prophet Jeremiah that He would make a New Covenant with His people. (*Jeremiah 31:31-34*)

- Jesus announced this New Covenant to His disciples at the Last Supper. (*1 Corinthians 11:23-25*)

- Today, all Christ-followers are required by God to live under the New Covenant or New Testament teachings.

  So the law was put in charge to lead us to Christ that we might be justified by faith. Now that faith has come, we are no longer under the supervision of the law (Galatians 3:24-25, NIV).

In a nutshell...

- The Bible is all about JESUS!

- The Old Testament is an account of one nation. The New Testament is an account of one Man. The nation was founded and nurtured by God to bring the Man into the world. His appearance on the earth is the central event of all history. The Old Testament sets the stage for it, the New Testament describes it.

- Since the Old Testament tells why God needed a plan to restore a relationship with the human race, and since the New Testament explains that Jesus was the plan, the point of the Bible can be summed up in one verse:

  For God so loved the world, that he gave his only Son, that whoever believes in him should not perish but have eternal life (John 3:16, ESV).

Biblical Timeline

2100 BC (about 4,100 years ago)   *God establishes a covenant with Abraham*

Abraham lived around 2100 BC in what is now Iraq. God told him to move to Canaan, which later became Israel. Unlike many people, Abraham believed in the one true God. God rewarded Abraham's faith, making him the father of a great nation (Israel), and an ancestor to the Messiah (Jesus Christ). *The Lord had said to Abram, "Go from your country, your people and your father's household to the land I will show you. I will make you into a great nation, and I will bless you; I will make your name great, and you will be a blessing. I will bless those who bless you, and whoever curses you I will curse; and all peoples on earth will be blessed through you" (Genesis 12:1-3, NIV).*

2000 BC (about 4,000 years ago)   *Jacob (Israel) is born*

Jacob, the son of Isaac, who was the son of Abraham, was born in Canaan. God changed Jacob's name to Israel. (Canaan is later renamed Israel, after Jacob). He had 12 sons, for whom the 12 Tribes of Israel were named: Gad, Asher, Reuben, Simeon, Levi, Judah, Issachar, Zebulun, Joseph, Benjamin, Dan, and Naphtali.

1900 BC (about 3,900 years ago)   *Joseph sold into slavery*

Joseph, one of Jacob's (Israel's) 12 sons, was sold into slavery by his brothers who were jealous of him. Joseph ended up in Egypt where he rose to power as a trusted assistant of a pharaoh. His father and brothers eventually left Canaan because of a great famine to go to Egypt where they were saved from harm by Joseph. *But Joseph said to them, "Don't be afraid. Am I in the place of God? You intended to harm me, but God intended it for good to accomplish what is now being done, the saving of lives" (Genesis 50:19, NIV).*

1446 BC (about 3,400 years ago)   *Exodus begins*

The Hebrews, or Israelites (descendants of Jacob), were enslaved for 400 years in Egypt until Moses led them out of Egypt. Because of their lack of faith, they wandered around in the desert for 40 years until Moses brought them to the border of Canaan, the land that God had previously promised to their forefather Abraham. *(Exodus 12:40)*

1406 BC (about 3,400 years ago)   *Israel becomes a sovereign country*

After Moses died, Joshua led the Israelites into Canaan and began conquering the land, establishing the sovereign country of Israel for the first time in history. (*Joshua 1:1-5*)

1400 BC (about 3,400 years ago)   *Israel is ruled by judges, not kings*

From about 1400 BC to 1050 BC, Israel was not ruled by kings, but instead, thought of God as their King and relied on judges to settle their disputes.

1050 BC (about 3,000 years ago)   *Saul becomes Israel's first king*

After about 350 years of being ruled by judges, the people of Israel demanded to have a king like their neighboring countries rather than trusting God as their King. Saul became king and reigned about 40 years.

1010 BC (about 3,000 years ago)   *David becomes King of Israel*

David became king of Israel around 1010 BC and reigned for 40 years. David, unlike Saul, followed the commands of God. He made mistakes, but he repented of them and sought to please God. He expanded the size of Israel and ruled over surrounding territories. David is known for being a man after God's own heart.

970 BC (about 3,000 years ago)   *Solomon becomes king, builds Temple*

Solomon, son of David, became king around 970 BC. He too reigned for about 40 years and built the Temple in honor of God. The work was completed around 960 BC, but Solomon eventually turned away from God and worshiped false gods.

926 BC (about 2,900 years ago)   *Israel becomes a divided kingdom*

Shortly after the reign of Solomon, Israel became a divided kingdom. The Southern Kingdom, called Judah, included the city of Jerusalem and the Temple. The Northern Kingdom continued to be called Israel, and the two were often at war with each other.

721 BC (about 2,700 years ago)   *Assyrians conquer northern kingdom of Israel*

The Assyrian Empire conquered the northern kingdom of Israel around 721 BC. The Assyrians tortured and decapitated many of the Israelites. They forced 10 of the 12 Tribes of Israel out of Israel and brought in foreigners. This was the beginning of what is known as the Exile.

612 BC (about 2,600 years ago)   ***Babylon conquers Nineveh (Assyrian Empire)***

The Assyrian Empire's capital city, Nineveh, was attacked by a coalition of Babylonians and others. As explained by the prophet Nahum, Nineveh was to be destroyed because of the Assyrian Empire's treatment of Israelites and other people.

605 BC (about 2,600 years ago)   ***Babylon exerts influence over Judah***

The neo-Babylonian Empire, under the reign of King Nebuchadnezzar, began forcing Judah into submission. Nebuchadnezzar took many Jews as captives to Babylon to ensure Judah's obedience.

597 BC (about 2,600 years ago)   ***Babylon attacks Judah***

The Babylonian army attacked Judah and took more Jews as captives to Babylon. Ezekiel, one of the captives, became a prophet of God. Ezekiel explained that God was allowing Babylon to punish Judah because the people had been unfaithful to Him.

586 BC (about 2,600 years ago)   ***Babylon destroys Jerusalem and the Temple***

Babylon attacked Judah again. This time, the Babylonians destroyed Jerusalem and the Temple that Solomon built, and more Jews were taken captive to Babylon.

539 BC (about 2,500 years ago)   ***Cyrus the Great conquers Babylon***

After the death of Nebuchadnezzar, the Neo-Babylonian Empire began to lose power. Cyrus the Great conquered Babylon in 539 BC, establishing the Medo-Persian Empire.

538 BC (about 2,500 years ago)   ***Cyrus releases Jews from Babylonian Captivity***

After conquering Babylon, Cyrus offered the Jews their freedom to leave Babylon and return to Judah. Cyrus' kingdom ruled over Judah and many other parts of the Middle East, but Cyrus allowed people more cultural and religious freedom than did the neo-Babylonian Empire.

536 BC (about 2,500 years ago)   ***Work begins to rebuild Temple***

Some of the Jews in Babylon returned to Judah and began work to rebuild the Temple that had been destroyed by the Babylonians in 586 BC.

516 BC (about 2,500 years ago)   *Second Temple is dedicated*

The Temple was consecrated for worship 70 years after the Babylonians had destroyed it.

333 BC (about 2,300 years ago)   *Greeks begin rule over land of Israel*

The Greeks, under the leadership of Alexander the Great, defeated Persian armies in Macedonia. This marked the fall of the Medo-Persian Empire and the rise of the Grecian Empire.

332 BC (about 2,300 years ago)   *Alexander conquers Tyre (Phoenician Empire)*

Alexander waged war against the island fortress of the Phoenician city of Tyre. He took rubble from the mainland of Tyre, built a walkway to the island, and then his forces conquered the island fortress bringing an end to the Phoenician Empire.

250 BC (about 2,300 years ago)   *The Old Testament was translated into Greek*

A Greek ruler asked the Jews to translate all or part of the Old Testament into the Greek language. The translation is called the Septuagint.

175 BC (about 2,200 years ago)   *Greek ruler Antiochus Epiphanes torments the Jews*

Greek ruler Antiochus Epiphanes, ruled Syria from about 175 BC to 164 BC. He reigned over Judah, defiled the Temple, and tried to destroy the Jewish religion.

164 BC to 63 BC (about 2,200 years ago)   *Jews have independence*

The Maccabees, a group of leaders of a Jewish rebel army, fought for Jewish independence, staged a revolt against the Greeks, and established the Hasmonean dynasty as well as sovereignty over all or part of the land of Israel for about 100 years.

63 BC (about 2,100 years ago)   *The Romans take over land of Israel*

After the death of Alexander the Great, the Greek Empire was divided up and became weaker, while the Roman Empire became increasingly more powerful, and the Roman general, Pompey, seized control over the land of Israel.

Around 5 BC (about 2,000 years ago)   *Jesus is born in Bethlehem*

Jesus was born in Bethlehem, which fulfilled a prophecy delivered by the prophet Micah about 700 years beforehand. (*Micah 5:2*)

About 25 AD (about 2,000 years ago)　　　　　　　　　　　　　*Jesus begins His ministry*

Jesus began His ministry when He was about 30 years old. He preached salvation, delivered prophecies, performed miracles, and announced He was the Messiah (the Christ) who was promised by the prophets of the Old Testament, bringing salvation and eternal life to those who believe in Him. (*John 3:16*)

About 28 AD (about 2,000 years ago)　　　　　　　*Jesus is crucified and resurrected*

Jesus was falsely accused of sedition against the Roman Empire and sent to Pontius Pilate, the Roman ruler of the land of the Jews, to be tried, convicted and crucified. But the Spirit of God raised Jesus from the dead, and His followers began evangelizing others, allowing Christianity to spread very quickly throughout the Roman Empire and eventually become the first religion to spread throughout the world.

70 AD (about 1,900 years ago)　　　　　　　*Romans destroy Jerusalem and Temple*

The Roman Army, under Titus, destroyed Jerusalem and the Temple to suppress an uprising of the Jews. It is estimated that about 1 million Jews were killed and others were taken as slaves.

First century AD (about 1,900 years ago)　　　　　　　　　*The Bible is completed*

The New Testament, which describes the life and teachings of Jesus Christ, was completed, and the writing of the Bible, which began about 3,400 years ago during the time of Moses, came to an end.

The Old Testament

39 books

Genesis, Exodus, Leviticus, Numbers, Deuteronomy, Joshua, Judges, Ruth, 1 Samuel, 2 Samuel, 1 Kings, 2 Kings, 1 Chronicles, 2 Chronicles, Ezra, Nehemiah, Esther, Job, Psalms, Proverbs, Ecclesiastes, Song of Solomon (also called Song of Songs), Isaiah, Jeremiah, Lamentations, Ezekiel, Daniel, Hosea, Joel, Amos, Obadiah, Jonah, Micah, Nahum, Habakkuk, Zephaniah, Haggai, Zechariah, Malachi

These books can be categorized as follows...

Pentateuch (Law) - 5 books
Genesis, Exodus, Leviticus, Numbers, and Deuteronomy

Historical Books - 12 books
Joshua, Judges, Ruth, 1 Samuel, 2 Samuel, 1 Kings, 2 Kings, 1 Chronicles, 2 Chronicles, Ezra, Nehemiah, Esther

Wisdom and Poetry - 5 books
Job, Psalms, Proverbs, Ecclesiastes, Song of Solomon

Prophetic - 17 books
Major Prophets - Isaiah, Jeremiah, Lamentations, Ezekiel, Daniel
Minor Prophets - Hosea, Joel, Amos, Obadiah, Jonah, Micah, Nahum, Habakkuk, Zephaniah, Haggai, Zechariah, Malachi

Summary of Books of the Old Testament

PENTATEUCH (First five books of the Old Testament—The Jewish Torah)

Genesis records the creation of the world by God, man's sinfulness and disobedience, and the earliest parts of God's plan to redeem mankind to Himself.

Exodus documents how God rescued Israel from Egypt and His instructions on how to act as a nation.

Leviticus contains God's instructions for Israel's priests and the entire nation on how to live spiritually and physically.

Numbers tells how God guaranteed the Israelites that the Promised Land would be theirs if they trusted Him, however, the Israelites initially refused to trust Him and were forced to wander in the wilderness for forty years until God gave them the opportunity to enter the Promised Land again.

Deuteronomy reminded the Israelites about what God had done for them, and encouraged them to devote their lives to Him. It is also a reminder to us that we should thank God for what He has done for us and dedicate our lives to Him.

HISTORICAL BOOKS

Joshua records the events of Israel's entrance into Canaan—the Promised Land.

Judges tells about Israel's persistent rebellion against God and the consequences, and how God called upon twelve human judges to deliver Israel from their sin and captivity during those years. It is also a reminder to us that God always judges sin and provides forgiveness for those who seek it.

Ruth is a book about loyalty, faith, and love of God and humanity and demonstrates how an individual can remain faithful to God even when the rest of the world is corrupt.

1 Samuel records the last days of the judges of Israel, the first days of the kings of Israel, and how Israel rejected God's leadership in favor of human leadership. It also reveals the stubbornness and evilness of the human heart and how God's true leadership should be followed.

2 Samuel documents the life and reign of David as Israel's king and how God called him a man after His own heart although he had committed numerous and despicable sins. It also shows us that although we too are full of sin, we can still return to God and lead a godly life.

1 Kings tells about the kings of the united kingdom of Israel and the divided kingdoms of Israel and Judah, most of whom were completely corrupt and led their kingdoms into sin. It also shows us the importance of godly leadership, and how God expects His leaders to take care of His people.

2 Kings tells about the prophets who were sent to warn the kings and people about impending judgment for both leaders and nations if they refused to repent of their sins and return to God, how the nations of Israel and Judah were destroyed and led into captivity because of their disobedience, and how important it is to make God the ultimate leader of our lives.

1 Chronicles details David's genealogy and summarizes the historical highlights of the kingdom of Israel. It also teaches us that God needs to be the center of our lives and is the only way to obtain eternal peace.

2 Chronicles teaches us that rejecting God leads to destruction while obeying Him leads to salvation, and uses the history of the good kings of Israel and Judah to show how deference to God brings prosperity, and the history of the evil kings of Israel to show how defiance of God leads to judgment.

Ezra tells about how God kept His promise to restore the Jews to their homeland and how the priest Ezra led the first wave of Jews back to Israel and initiated the process of rebuilding their nation.

Nehemiah is the final Old Testament history book that records the events of the third wave of Jews to return to Israel and shows how God can use one man to accomplish His purposes.

Esther is an intriguing story of faith, courage, obedience, drama and romance, and although never mentions God by name, overwhelmingly shows that His Spirit is ever present and that His will shall always be done regardless of human plans.

WISDOM AND POETRY

Job teaches us that God is sovereign, the causes of suffering are not always known, people who follow God are not immune from suffering, and we cannot fully understand the mind of God.

Psalms is a poetic book of praise and worship to God and shows that the supreme purpose for man's existence is to exalt and give thanks to God.

Proverbs is a book of wisdom for everyday life that tells us that the source of wisdom is God and that it is folly to look to anyone or anything else for truth.

Ecclesiastes teaches us that life is meaningless without God and contains much sadness, but those who believe and trust in God will ultimately be fulfilled.

Song of Solomon is a book that symbolically demonstrates God's love for His people; literally expresses the physical and emotional love between a man and a woman; poetically and graphically tells how physical and emotional love should be handled in courtship and marriage; and stresses that physical love is proper and God-ordained when confined to the oneness of marriage.

MAJOR PROPHETS

Isaiah warned the people of Israel that they must either turn from their sins or else face the judgment of God; foretold the coming of the Messiah as the ultimate sacrifice for all mankind validating the truthfulness of the Bible; and shows us that we need to follow God in our lives.

Jeremiah warned the people of Israel to repent of their sins and to ask God for His forgiveness and reminds us that even when no one will listen to His truth, we should still proclaim it.

Lamentations shows God's sorrow over the nation of Israel's sin, how we sadden Him and pave the way for self-destruction when we reject Him, and how true love cares for others.

Ezekiel warned the Israelites who were living in exile to repent of their sins, and it is also an encouragement to us that when we are in the midst of our enemies or experiencing trying times, we should hold fast to the word of God and share His truth with others.

Daniel teaches us that we can serve God and be successful even when we are at the mercy of an immoral world and a corrupt society, and that we should never abandon our faith in God, even when our personal safety is endangered.

MINOR PROPHETS

Hosea is an allegorical and literal book about the love, commitment, and forgiveness of a prophet to his unfaithful wife and shows us how God forgives us when we commit adultery against Him by putting anything other than Him first in our lives.

Joel pronounced God's impending judgment for those who refused to leave their sinful life and shows us that there is mercy for those who repent and turn to God.

Amos tells us to be bold in declaring God's truth, even when it means risking our personal freedom or reputation and shows us how ordinary people can be used by God for His purposes; no one is too small to do His work.

Obadiah pronounced judgment against those who harm God's people and shows us that God cares for those who follow Him.

Jonah teaches us that we cannot escape God if He calls us to do His work and that He will not let evil go unpunished but is eager to forgive those who repent.

Micah shows us that God does not tolerate wicked behavior and that those who believe their actions have no consequences will eventually be destroyed, but He also offers forgiveness to those who ask Him for it and are willing to forsake their evil ways to follow Him.

Nahum shows us that even the mightiest of people and nations are not immune from God's judgment and power, and that He will defend His people and wipe out those who oppose Him.

Habakkuk offers hope to people in their time of need and shows us that even though evil often appears to rule the world, God is really in control.

Zephaniah urges people to follow God even when they experience times of prosperity, and also shows us that we are not responsible for our own wellbeing and will experience judgment when we ignore God in times of peace and affluence.

Haggai tells about the people of Israel, who after returning to their homeland from exile, were living in luxury and had forgotten that it was God who had freed them, and also challenges us to put God first in our lives.

Zechariah predicts the life of Christ and shows us that we are eternally saved because of Christ's sacrifice on the Cross and resurrection from the dead.

Malachi is the final book of the Old Testament that foretells the birth of Christ, warns people to let go of their evil desires, and to follow God.

The New Testament

27 Books

Matthew, Mark, Luke, John, Acts of the Apostles, Romans, 1 Corinthians, 2 Corinthians, Galatians, Ephesians, Philippians, Colossians, 1 Thessalonians, 2 Thessalonians, 1 Timothy, 2 Timothy, Titus, Philemon, Hebrews, James, 1 Peter, 2 Peter, 1 John, 2 John, 3 John, Jude, Revelation

These books can be categorized as follows...

The Gospels - 4 books
Matthew, Mark, Luke, John

Historical Book
Acts

Paul's Letters - 13 books
Romans, 1 Corinthians, 2 Corinthians, Galatians, Ephesians, Philippians, Colossians, 1 Thessalonians, 2 Thessalonians, 1 Timothy, 2 Timothy, Titus, Philemon

Non-Pauline Letters (General Letters) - 8 books
Hebrews, James, 1 Peter, 2 Peter, 1 John, 2 John, 3 John, Jude

Apocalyptic
Revelation

Summary of the Books of New Testament

THE GOSPELS

Matthew is the first of the four Gospels that covers the life, teachings, death and resurrection of Jesus Christ, God incarnate, portrays Jesus as King, and gives us practical ways to live in His kingdom today through His teachings.

Mark is the second Gospel and focuses on the actions of Jesus; who He was and His teachings, works, and miracles. Mark begins by showing that Jesus fulfilled the predictions made hundreds of years earlier by the prophet Isaiah.

Luke is the third Gospel and presents the most exhaustive account of Jesus' life and death and includes many accounts of the women He interacted with; affirms the dual aspects of Jesus' human and divine nature; and teaches that Jesus is the only way to heaven and that no one can earn their salvation.

John is the fourth Gospel and is unique compared to the other Gospels by focusing on Jesus as God and that He has always existed; that Jesus is the Son of God and the only way to eternal salvation; that Jesus' death and resurrection provides our salvation from eternal damnation; and that all must believe He paid the price for their sins, confess they are sinners, and ask for and receive His forgiveness in order to go to heaven.

HISTORICAL

Acts begins where the Gospels end, and tells about the early Christian church and spreading of the Gospel message.

PAULINE LETTERS

Romans is a message about salvation available to all who accept God's grace and that people are destined for destruction unless they accept the forgiveness that is not deserved.

1 Corinthians reveals some problems in the early Christian church, how to avoid similar problems, and how to lead a holy life in an unholy world.

2 Corinthians teaches that the Christian faith will be attacked and we must be ready to defend what we believe and profess and also be careful that what we believe and profess is truthful.

Galatians teaches that customs and rituals are not necessary for salvation and that customs and rituals do not provide salvation.

Ephesians tells about the purpose of the Church; a united body of believers who strengthen each other and perform community worship and service to God.

Philippians celebrates the joy that Christians should have and the reasons to praise God.

Colossians refutes false teachings in the church and shows us that Christ is the supreme head of His Church and that all truth comes from Him.

1 Thessalonians teaches Christians to be strong in their faith in times of persecution and tells about the second coming of Christ and how we should prepare for it.

2 Thessalonians provides more information on the second coming of Christ and tells us that although Christ could return at any moment, no one knows when that moment will be.

1 Timothy gives instructions to church leaders and teaches how to administer and discipline a church.

2 Timothy is the Apostle Paul's final letter before His death that further instructs church leaders and encourages Christians in their walk with Christ.

Titus contains more instructions from Paul on how to be a good leader and a good Christian, how to avoid the pitfalls of faith, and how to be responsible and moral at all times.

Philemon reaffirms that all people are equal in God's eyes and that Christians especially should treat those who may be viewed by others as inferior with respect and fairness.

NON-PAULINE LETTERS

Hebrews presents Christianity as the only true faith, Christ as all we need for our salvation, how Jesus fulfills the Old Testament Covenant, and that we must put our trust in God.

James is a book that warns us to beware of hypocrisy, in others and in ourselves, and teaches us how to live the true Christian life.

1 Peter encourages Christians who are suffering persecution and difficult times, that although we may face earthly pain and suffering, we will find eternal peace if we put our faith in God.

2 Peter warns us to beware of false teachings and tells us that we have a responsibility to grow in our faith and knowledge of God.

1 John defends Christianity, cautions us to watch for people who try to lead us astray, and teaches us what our relationship with God should be.

2 John tells us to be wary of deceivers and emphasizes that Christians should live a life of truth and love.

3 John shows how simple acts of kindness, such as hospitality, should be a part of the Christian's walk with God, and how we should be sure to walk according to the true Gospel and not according to those who hinder God's work.

Jude warns us that we must never let our guard down and that we always need to be on the lookout for heretics and false teachings.

APOCALYPTIC

Revelation completes God's revealed Word to His people and is full of symbols and imagery describing what is yet to come when Jesus returns to judge the world in righteousness, destroy all wickedness for all eternity, and establish His never ending kingdom.

Background on the Book of Philippians

The Apostle Paul's letter to believers in Philippi is known as the most tender of all his letters, so it comes as a surprise that he wrote this letter while imprisoned in Rome! The church at Philippi was founded during Paul's second missionary journey to Asia Minor. Soon after Paul and his missionary companion, Silas, arrived at Philippi, they met a group of women having a prayer meeting by a riverside and shared the Gospel with them. Lydia, one of the women, received Paul's message and she and the members of her household were baptized. Then she invited them into her home where she displayed great hospitality and kindness (see Acts 16). So, the Philippian church began in a woman's home. How great is that!

Paul's preaching in the city stirred up a lot of opposition. Before long, Paul and Silas found themselves arrested, severely flogged, and thrown into jail with their legs fastened in stocks. However, this did not seem to inhibit the faith of these radical followers of Christ. Instead, they looked at this situation as an opportunity to pray and sing praises to God despite their dire circumstances, and as the other prisoners were listening to them, a great earthquake shook so violently that the prison doors flew open. Seeing the prison doors open, and knowing that the punishment for letting prisoners escape was death, the jailer prepared to take his own life. Paul stopped the frightened jailer and assured him that all the prisoners were still in their cells. The jailer looked up at Paul and Silas and must have been so impressed by their kindness and grace that he immediately wanted the kind of life they had and asked them what he must do to be saved. Like Lydia, the jailer and his household received Paul's salvation message and were baptized and Paul and Silas were soon let go.

Years later, sometime between 60-62 AD, Paul was imprisoned in Rome under house arrest while awaiting an ominous trial before the Roman emperor Nero (see Acts 28). Epaphroditus, a man from the church at Philippi, visited him bringing him gifts and offering support and care. This visit reminded Paul of his beloved friends in Philippi and prompted him to write a letter to them to show his appreciation and love for them and thank them for their continued help and support and also to encourage them in their spiritual growth.

Paul was chained day and night to a Roman soldier and he was suffering and facing possible death, yet he chose to be an encouragement to others and wrote his letter with sincerity, confidence, strength, and joy. Because the church in Philippi was experiencing the normal problems of everyday life, Paul focused on offering them guidance for everyday living.

Paul walked personally and intimately with Jesus Christ. He knew that Christ was with him through all the highs and lows of his ministry and Christ was the help he turned to in all things. Paul's letter is such an encouragement to us that no matter what each day may bring, we can, like Paul, with Christ and the power of the Holy Spirit, live victoriously and joyfully in the midst of pain and suffering or any difficulty that may come our way!

Lesson One: *Joy in Being an Encourager* (Philippians 1:1-11)

𝓕   *Focus on the Passage*

Philippians Chapter 1:1-11 (ESV)

1 Paul and Timothy, servants of Christ Jesus,

To all the saints in Christ Jesus who are at Philippi, with the overseers and deacons:

2 Grace to you and peace from God our Father and the Lord Jesus Christ.

3 I thank my God in all my remembrance of you,

4 always in every prayer of mine for you all making my prayer with joy,

5 because of your partnership in the gospel from the first day until now.

6 And I am sure of this, that he who began a good work in you will bring it to completion at the day of Jesus Christ.

7 It is right for me to feel this way about you all, because I hold you in my heart, for you are all partakers with me of grace, both in my imprisonment and in the defense and confirmation of the gospel.

8 For God is my witness, how I yearn for you all with the affection of Christ Jesus.

9 And it is my prayer that your love may abound more and more, with knowledge and all discernment,

1. *Ask God to open your mind and heart to receive His truth and the Holy Spirit to be your guide.*

2. *Read the passage 2-3 times.*

As you read, ask yourself...

3. *What is going on in the passage (5 W's & H)?*

4. *What are the repeated words or contrasts?*

5. *What are the natural divisions in the passage?*

6. *What is the theme?*

7. *What questions do you have?*

8. *What word(s) bring you comfort?*

9. *What truth(s) are you having a hard time accepting?*

10. *What are you thankful for?*

10 so that you may approve what is excellent, and so be pure and blameless for the day of Christ,

11 filled with the fruit of righteousness that comes through Jesus Christ, to the glory and praise of God.

A   *Admit Where You Are*

1. Define "joy" in your own words. How is joy different than happiness?

2. List the things in your life that give you joy?

3. What are your "joy robbers?" Do you often find yourself waiting for those things to be removed from your life before you can be joyful?

4. Do you consider yourself a spiritually minded person? Why or why not?

5. What is true Christian fellowship?

6. Why is forgiveness one of the most difficult but significant evidences of genuine love between Christians?

7. How can praying for other Christians improve our fellowship with them?

8. Are you able to be grateful for the blessings others receive even when you are in a place of difficulty?

I   *Interpret the Passage*

Paul provides us with an incredible model on how to encourage others. We don't have to wait to be in a good place either to do it. Not only is encouragement good for others, but God also encourages us in the process. As Paul wrote this letter to the Philippians, his heart was encouraged as he remembered the friendships and the history he had with this church.

1. Looking at Philippians 1:1-11, identify key facts about the *who, what, where, when, why and how* of this passage.

2. Using a Bible dictionary define "sanctification." Who does the work of sanctification? What is our role? (see Romans 6:6, 1 Corinthians 6:11, Romans 12:1-2, and 2 Peter 3:18).

3. Often the best way to influence the lives of others is to pray for them. Write out Paul's prayer in Philippians 1:9-11.

    *   What is the focus of Paul's prayer?

    *   What do you learn about what to pray for others?

    *   Are there people in your life who would benefit from this type of prayer? Read Philippians 1:9-11 aloud inserting their names and praying accordingly.

4. In Philippians 1:11, Paul prayed that the Philippians would be filled with the *"fruit of righteousness."* What do you think the fruit of righteousness is?

- Read Galatians 5:22-23. What do these verses add to your understanding of what the "fruit of righteousness" looks like?

- How does being fruitful bring joy?

5. Paul revealed the secret to joy in the first 11 verses of this letter. Go back and find examples for the following:

- Being other's focused.

- Being grateful for all things.

- Being trusting of God for the ways He is completing you.

- Being in God's Word.

- Being in prayer.

𝒯 *Take This Passage into Your Life*

1. Paul loved the Philippians with Jesus' affection. How would your life or attitude change this week if you were fully convinced that God loves you because He enjoys you?

2. The disenchantment of our own abilities is, perhaps, one of the most important things that can ever happen to us. Do you agree? Why or why not?

3. 1 Corinthians 10:13 (ESV) says, *No temptation has overtaken you that is not common to man. God is faithful, and he will not let you be tempted beyond your ability, but with the temptation he will also provide the way of escape, that you may be able to endure it.* Do you find yourself in a season or situation where your circumstances seem beyond what you can handle? How might God be using your places of difficulty to reveal to you that apart from Him you can't handle much, but when you are dependent on Him, He can handle all of it?

4. Turn to your Journey Journal and write down those things that seem overwhelming and out of your control. By faith, claim that God is sovereign and knows exactly what He is doing in your life. Practice shifting your eyes off your circumstances and onto the Lord this week.

5. Spend a few minutes in prayer surrendering those people, things, or circumstances that are keeping you focused on yourself. Ask God to help you remember that with His help, you can begin to see your life through His eyes again.

6. Despite Paul's dreadful circumstances, he was able to focus on others by taking his eyes off himself. He didn't ask the Philippians to pray for him and his situation but instead he prayed for them. Why might this practice be helpful for us as well?

7. Reach out to a friend in your Faith Journey group and ask for prayer that you would be able to keep your focus on God and on encouraging and serving others this week.

8. If you find yourself in a season of great difficulty, what encouragement from Paul's example in Philippians 1:1-11 can you apply to your life?

9. Psalm 68:3 (ESV) says, *But the righteous shall be glad; they shall exult before God; they shall be jubilant with joy!* Joy is what happens to us when we allow ourselves to recognize how good things really are. Be sure to take time this week to shout out to God all the things you are grateful for and for the gifts He has given specifically to you.

10. How can Philippians 1:1-11 prepare you for an unexpected crisis? What is your Biblical game plan in the event of an emergency in your faith journey?

Happiness depends on happenings. Joy depends on Christ!

ℋ   Hear from God

1. How is God speaking to me through this passage?

2. What promises do I need to claim?

3. What are the things I can thank God for? Take time to thank Him.

4. What is God convicting me of that I need to change? Is there a sin to confess?

5. Who is God prompting me to pray for in response to this week's study?

6. What special truth did God teach me that I would like to share with others?

Journey Challenge

This week memorize Philippians 1:6

And I am sure of this, that he who began a good work in you will bring it to completion at the day of Jesus Christ.

Lesson Two: *Joy in Our Chains* (Philippians 1:12-30)

ℱ *Focus on the Passage*

Philippians Chapter 1:12-30 (ESV)

12 I want you to know, brothers, that what has happened to me has really served to advance the gospel,

13 so that it has become known throughout the whole imperial guard and to all the rest that my imprisonment is for Christ.

14 And most of the brothers, having become confident in the Lord by my imprisonment, are much more bold to speak the word without fear.

15 Some indeed preach Christ from envy and rivalry, but others from good will.

16 The latter do it out of love, knowing that I am put here for the defense of the gospel.

17 The former proclaim Christ out of selfish ambition, not sincerely but thinking to afflict me in my imprisonment.

18 What then? Only that in every way, whether in pretense or in truth, Christ is proclaimed, and in that I rejoice.

Yes, and I will rejoice,

19 for I know that through your prayers and the help of the Spirit of Jesus Christ this will turn out for my deliverance,

1. Ask God to open your mind and heart to receive His truth and the Holy Spirit to be your guide.

2. Read the passage 2-3 times.

As you read, ask yourself...

3. What is going on in the passage (5 W's & H)?

4. What are the repeated words or contrasts?

5. What are the natural divisions in the passage?

6. What is the theme?

7. What questions do you have?

8. What word(s) bring you comfort?

9. What truth(s) are you having a hard time accepting?

10. What are you thankful for?

20 as it is my eager expectation and hope that I will not be at all ashamed, but that with full courage now as always Christ will be honored in my body, whether by life or by death.

21 For to me to live is Christ, and to die is gain.

22 If I am to live in the flesh, that means fruitful labor for me. Yet which I shall choose I cannot tell.

23 I am hard pressed between the two. My desire is to depart and be with Christ, for that is far better.

24 But to remain in the flesh is more necessary on your account.

25 Convinced of this, I know that I will remain and continue with you all, for your progress and joy in the faith,

26 so that in me you may have ample cause to glory in Christ Jesus, because of my coming to you again.

27 Only let your manner of life be worthy of the gospel of Christ, so that whether I come and see you or am absent, I may hear of you that you are standing firm in one spirit, with one mind striving side by side for the faith of the gospel,

28 and not frightened in anything by your opponents. This is a clear sign to them of their destruction, but of your salvation, and that from God.

29 For it has been granted to you that for the sake of Christ you should not only believe in him but also suffer for his sake,

30 engaged in the same conflict that you saw I had and now hear that I still have.

A   *Admit Where You Are*

1. Do you look at difficulty in your life as opportunities to minister to others or as things that hold you back?

2. How can Christ be magnified through a crisis in your life?

3. What kind of chains in your life has Christ used to impact others?

4. How does going through spiritual conflict help us grow?

5. Can you look back on a season in your life where you experienced spiritual growth as a result of hardship? Explain how that happened.

6. What are the ways you cope with stress apart from God? How is that working for you?

7. God often tests our faith to show us our weaknesses and to make us spiritually stronger. List an example from your own life of the good God has brought out of your suffering.

I   *Interpret the Passage*

Paul knew that the prayers of the believers in Philippi and the Spirit of Jesus Christ enabled him to be free from self-interest while he was in prison and to be bold and unashamed of defending the gospel of Christ. His greatest concern was that Christ be honored in his body regardless of what awaited him, even if it was in death. There was no wavering in Paul's spirit, only openness to fulfill the will of God.

It's easy to approach a passage like this and excuse ourselves from having an attitude like Paul's. Some might even shrug it off thinking; "It makes sense for great men and women of the Bible and spiritual leaders in history to be completely sold out for Christ but not me." The enemy tries to prevent us from knowing and believing that we can have the same attitude and determination as Paul to glorify Christ no matter how difficult our circumstances, but he is a liar! The truth is we have the same Spirit of Christ living in us who gives us the desire and the courage to speak the Word of God without fear.

Philippians 1:21 (ESV) says, *For to me to live is Christ, and to die is gain.* This verse was the basis for Paul's ability to live victoriously in Christ. He was not concerned about drawing attention to himself; rather he wanted to glorify Jesus Christ in everything he said and did. His entire life was focused on Jesus.

1. Looking at Philippians 1:12-30, identify key facts about the *who, what, where, when, why and how* of this passage.

2. Read Philippians 1:12. More than anything, Paul's desire as a missionary was to preach the Gospel in Rome, the hub of the great Roman Empire. However, Paul's plan was interrupted by his imprisonment. Did this stop him from achieving his goal? How did God use Paul's chains to advance the Gospel?

3. Genesis 50:20 (NIV) says, *You intended to harm me, but God intended it for good to accomplish what is now being done, the saving of many lives.* What do we learn about God from this verse and how He sometimes works in our lives?

4. Read Philippians 1:12-14 and make the following observations:

   - What was Paul choosing to focus on?

   - What was he refusing to do?

5. In Philippians 1:15-19, Paul says that the Gospel is being preached. Some preach out of love and others with wrong motives. What was Paul's reaction to those who were preaching with wrong motives?

   - Why do you think Paul brought this up to the Philippians?

   - What good was Paul focusing on?

6. Read Philippians 1:20-26 and summarize Paul's heart and motivation for living.

7. Write out the following verses on why we are called to unity as believers:

   - 1 Corinthians 1:10

   - Ephesians 4:1-3

- Colossians 3:14

8. Why is it important for Christians to maintain unity?

9. Paul considered his suffering a great privilege. Read through the following verses and list the benefits we receive when we endure suffering.

Count it all joy, my brothers, when you meet trials of various kinds, for you know that the testing of your faith produces steadfastness. And let steadfastness have its full effect, that you may be perfect and complete, lacking in nothing. James 1:2-4 (ESV)

For I consider that the sufferings of this present time are not worth comparing with the glory that is to be revealed to us. Romans 8:18 (ESV)

For the sake of Christ, then, I am content with weaknesses, insults, hardships, persecutions, and calamities. For when I am weak, then I am strong. 2 Corinthians 12:10 (ESV)

We are afflicted in every way, but not crushed; perplexed, but not driven to despair; persecuted, but not forsaken; struck down, but not destroyed; always carrying in the body the death of Jesus, so that the life of Jesus may also be manifested in our bodies. For we who live are always being given over to death for Jesus' sake, so that the life of Jesus also may be manifested in our mortal flesh. 2 Corinthians 4:8-11 (ESV)

T   *Take This Passage into Your Life*

1. Psalm 16:11 (NIV) says, *You make known to me the path of life; you will fill me with joy in your presence, with eternal pleasures at your right hand.* Even when things do not make sense, God uses our places of unknown to make Himself known to us. What steps can you take this week to stay connected to God as you deal with your unknowns?

2. There are opportunities for Christ's power to be magnified in us during times of crisis. According to Nehemiah 8:10 (ESV), *The joy of the Lord is your strength.* In what ways do you see God working in you to bring good out of difficult circumstances?

    *   In what ways can you show others His power working in your faith through difficulty?

3. Paul said, *"For to me to live is Christ, and to die is gain"* (1:21). What does this verse mean to you?

    *   In what ways can you apply Paul's attitude towards your circumstances this week?

    *   Do you have fears about being sold out for Christ like Paul was? What are they?

4. We cannot control our circumstances, however, we can control our response to them. We have a choice. What does it mean to *let your manner of life be worthy of the gospel of Christ* (1:27a)?

5. Meditate on Isaiah 43:1-4. What assurances and encouragement does this passage provide you with when facing difficult circumstances?

6. What activities are you doing to further your own interests rather than furthering God's plan for your life?

   • What steps can you take in your faith journey to trust God with His best interest for you?

Our problems are opportunities to discover God's solutions!

_H_ _Hear from God_

1. How is God speaking to me through this passage?

2. What promises do I need to claim?

3. What are the things I can thank God for? Take time to thank Him.

4. What is God convicting me of that I need to change? Is there a sin to confess?

5. Who is God prompting me to pray for in response to this week's study?

6. What special truth did God teach me that I would like to share with others?

Journey Challenge

This week memorize Philippians 1:21

For to me to live is Christ, and to die is gain.

Lesson Three: *Joy in Serving* (Philippians 2:1-11)

𝓕 Focus on the Passage

Philippians Chapter 2:1-11 (ESV)

1 So if there is any encouragement in Christ, any comfort from love, any participation in the Spirit, any affection and sympathy,

2 complete my joy by being of the same mind, having the same love, being in full accord and of one mind.

3 Do nothing from selfish ambition or conceit, but in humility count others more significant than yourselves.

4 Let each of you look not only to his own interests, but also to the interests of others.

5 Have this mind among yourselves, which is yours in Christ Jesus,

6 who, though he was in the form of God, did not count equality with God a thing to be grasped,

7 but emptied himself, by taking the form of a servant, being born in the likeness of men.

8 And being found in human form, he humbled himself by becoming obedient to the point of death, even death on a cross.

9 Therefore God has highly exalted him and bestowed on him the name that is above every name,

1. Ask God to open your mind and heart to receive His truth and the Holy Spirit to be your guide.

2. Read the passage 2-3 times.

As you read, ask yourself...

3. What is going on in the passage (5 W's & H)?

4. What are the repeated words or contrasts?

5. What are the natural divisions in the passage?

6. What is the theme?

7. What questions do you have?

8. What word(s) bring you comfort?

9. What truth(s) are you having a hard time accepting?

10. What are you thankful for?

10 so that at the name of Jesus every knee should bow, in heaven and on earth and under the earth,

11 and every tongue confess that Jesus Christ is Lord, to the glory of God the Father.

$\mathcal{A}$ *Admit Where You Are*

I have a dear friend who has been battling chronic pain from Rheumatoid Arthritis. Health issues have been her greatest source of suffering for many years. In the past year alone, she has undergone four surgeries. However, through the pain the fruit of her faith has grown even greater. Chronic pain is one of the top challenges people face and the prospects of waking up each day with a debilitating condition without any reprieve in sight truly tests one's faith.

My friend told me about an amazing opportunity she had one Christmas to serve her neighbors. She was recovering from surgery and in a great deal of pain, but the Lord had put it on her heart to reach out to her 85 year old neighbor and her neighbor's adult son. The son had made some poor choices a few years earlier and was under scrutiny and rejection by the neighborhood. Although judgment was upon him, God's grace was on my friend as she reached out to him.

As I listened intensely to my friend talk about the blessings she received from sharing Christ's love, I became aware of how unhindered she was by her recovery. She had every excuse in the world to be served and cared for, but she put her needs aside and served her neighbors' needs instead and being used by God in this way was the greatest gift she received that Christmas.

Every day we have opportunities to ask God, "Who can I serve?" Through prayer, His Spirit enables us to have gracious and loving eyes to see the brokenness in others. And the blessings we receive as we become vessels God uses to serve and care for others are truly blessings from heaven! We are told in Isaiah 55:12 (NLT) that when we seek God and do the things of God, we *will live in joy and peace. The mountains and hills will burst into song, and the trees of the field will clap their hands!*

1. Do you have people in your life who are difficult to serve? What about them makes serving them difficult?

2. What words or thoughts come to mind when you read or hear the word submissive?

3. How does selfish ambition rob us of the joy that comes from serving others?

4. We often tend to serve when it is convenient. Why are we prone to serve those who are "easy" to serve? What blessings might we receive when we serve those we consider difficult?

5. As Christians, we are called to have the same attitude as Christ did. What fears do you have about laying down your rights?

6. Why do you think the road of humility less traveled?

I can rejoice in spite of my circumstances because my circumstances strengthen and promote the furtherance of the Gospel!

I   *Interpret the Passage*

In Philippians chapter one, Paul reveals how to be joyful in all circumstances and encourages us to stand strong against any external difficulty we may face. Now, in chapter two, Paul shows us how to respond to internal conflicts within the body of Christ. There is no greater roadblock to sharing the gospel to the watching world than Christians not getting along with each other!

Now I don't know about you but when I come to a passage like this I am tempted to think, "Well, he doesn't know my situation. He just doesn't know how much...

> I've tried to reconcile with others.
> I serve my children with little response.
> I disagree with my husband (and think God would too).
> I've tried to reach out to friends without success.
> I put everyone else's needs above my own and get nothing in return."

Maybe you have relationships that have caused hurt, misunderstanding or division and you're thinking, "Yeah, Paul you don't know ME." I believe Paul knew exactly how we would react to his exhortations to *do nothing from selfish ambition or conceit, but in humility count others more significant than yourselves* (v4) and *let each of you look not only to his own interests, but also to the interests of others* (v5). So, Paul starts out by getting us to take stock of what we have because of our personal relationship with Jesus Christ. Then he gives us an incredible model of how to be a true and humble servant by following our greatest example, Jesus Christ.

Imagine what would happen if we applied Philippians 2:1-11 to the ways we relate to each other in this group, in our churches, in our marriages, in our families, in the places we work, or where ever we go!

1. Looking at Philippians 2:1-12, identify key facts about the *who, what, where, when, why and how* of this passage.

2. Read Philippians 2:1 and list four wonderful things that are ours in Christ.

3. Ephesians 4:1-6 (NIV) says, *As a prisoner for the Lord, then, I urge you to live a life worthy of the calling you have received. Be completely humble and gentle; be patient, bearing with one another in love. Make every effort to keep the unity of the Spirit through the bond of peace. There is one body and one Spirit, just as you were called to one hope when you were called; one Lord, one faith, one baptism; one God and Father of all, who is over all and through all and in all.*

- What does it mean to be a prisoner for the Lord?

- What rights must one give up to follow Christ?

- What are the results when we live our lives *"worthy of the calling?"*

4. Paul was already experiencing joy in prison as he wrote this letter. But in this passage, Paul says his joy overflows when believers all get along and are unified in purpose and attitude. If you are a parent, you understand how sweet it is when your kids all get along. Write out the following verses and what you learn about living in harmony with one another.

- Romans 12:16

- Romans 15:5-6

- 1 Corinthians 1:10

5. There is conflict in the world because we are conflicted people. At the root of conflict is always pride and self-centeredness. *What causes fights and quarrels among you? Don't they come from your desires that battle within you? You desire but do not have, so you kill. You covet but you cannot get what you want, so you quarrel and fight. You do not have because you do not ask God. When you ask, you do not receive, because you ask with wrong motives, that you may spend what you get on your pleasures. James 4:1-3 (NIV)* What is Paul's solution for handling conflict in Philippians 2:3-4?

6. When conflict entered the world, it would have been easier for God to avoid us all together or just start over. But instead, Jesus, God's son, left His place on the throne in heaven and became a man. Not a rich man or powerful king, but a poor carpenter. He didn't say: "I have my rights;" "I have my self-respect;" "I deserve better than this;" "These people don't appreciate me." Instead, He emptied Himself of all His rights and became a servant for you and me. Read Philippians 2:6-11 and underline everything this passage has to say about:

   • True servanthood?

   • Demanding our rights?

7. 1 Peter 2:24 (NIV) says, *"He himself bore our sins" in his body on the cross, so that we might die to sins and live for righteousness; "by his wounds you have been healed."* What does this verse mean to you?

$\mathcal{T}$ *Take This Passage into Your Life*

1. Joy is complete when we get along with each other. Are there any challenging relationships in your life that would benefit from steps you can take to apply Philippians 2:1 this week?

2. Do you have a situation in your life right now where the Lord is asking you to lay down your rights first? Do you desire to do this? What are you afraid of?

3. Spend a few minutes asking the Holy Spirit to give you God's desire for those people He is asking you to serve, recognizing that you are just the vehicle or the mouthpiece for Him to work through.

4. Romans 12:3 (NIV) says, *For by the grace given me I say to every one of you: Do not think of yourself more highly than you ought, but rather think of yourself with sober judgment, in accordance with the faith God has distributed to each of you.* What is true humility? What practical things can you do to become more humble in your everyday life?

5. How is pride our greatest spiritual defeat? Take a few minutes to confess those areas of your life where pride is preventing you from receiving God's grace.

6. Do you feel that you are owed anything right now? Surrender your bitterness and martyrdom to God right now and allow His peace and understanding to fill you in a new way this week.

7. How might each day look different if you followed Jesus' example every time you had a choice to make?

There is no greater roadblock to sharing the gospel to the watching world than Christians not getting along with each other!

𝓗   Hear from God

1. How is God speaking to me through this passage?

2. What promises do I need to claim?

3. What are the things I can thank God for? Take time to thank Him.

4. What is God convicting me of that I need to change? Is there a sin to confess?

5. Who is God prompting me to pray for in response to this week's study?

6. What special truth did God teach me that I would like to share with others?

Journey Challenge

This week memorize Philippians 2:3

Do nothing from selfish ambition or conceit, but in humility count others more significant than yourselves.

Lesson Four: *Joy in Obedience* (Philippians 2:12-30)

𝓕   *Focus on the Passage*

Philippians Chapter 2:12-30 (ESV)

12 Therefore, my beloved, as you have always obeyed, so now, not only as in my presence but much more in my absence, work out your own salvation with fear and trembling,

13 for it is God who works in you, both to will and to work for his good pleasure.

14 Do all things without grumbling or disputing,

15 that you may be blameless and innocent, children of God without blemish in the midst of a crooked and twisted generation, among whom you shine as lights in the world,

16 holding fast to the word of life, so that in the day of Christ I may be proud that I did not run in vain or labor in vain.

17 Even if I am to be poured out as a drink offering upon the sacrificial offering of your faith, I am glad and rejoice with you all.

18 Likewise you also should be glad and rejoice with me.

19 I hope in the Lord Jesus to send Timothy to you soon, so that I too may be cheered by news of you.

20 For I have no one like him, who will be genuinely concerned for your welfare.

1. Ask God to open your mind and heart to receive His truth and the Holy Spirit to be your guide.

2. Read the passage 2-3 times.

As you read, ask yourself...

3. What is going on in the passage (5 W's & H)?

4. What are the repeated words or contrasts?

5. What are the natural divisions in the passage?

6. What is the theme?

7. What questions do you have?

8. What word(s) bring you comfort?

9. What truth(s) are you having a hard time accepting?

10. What are you thankful for?

21 For they all seek their own interests, not those of Jesus Christ.

22 But you know Timothy's proven worth, how as a son with a father he has served with me in the gospel.

23 I hope therefore to send him just as soon as I see how it will go with me,

24 and I trust in the Lord that shortly I myself will come also.

25 I have thought it necessary to send to you Epaphroditus my brother and fellow worker and fellow soldier, and your messenger and minister to my need,

26 for he has been longing for you all and has been distressed because you heard that he was ill.

27 Indeed he was ill, near to death. But God had mercy on him, and not only on him but on me also, lest I should have sorrow upon sorrow.

28 I am the more eager to send him, therefore, that you may rejoice at seeing him again, and that I may be less anxious.

29 So receive him in the Lord with all joy, and honor such men,

30 for he nearly died for the work of Christ, risking his life to complete what was lacking in your service to me.

A   Admit Where You Are

1. How does having a complaining or argumentative attitude hinder our relationship with God and others?

2. In what ways do you feel like your faith goes up and down? What keeps you from living a consistent faith?

3. What are your greatest challenges to being Christ-like in your:

    *   Attitude?

    *   Perspective?

    *   Behavior?

4. 1 Peter 1:8-9 (ESV) says, *Though you have not seen him, you love him. Though you do not now see him, you believe in him and rejoice with joy that is inexpressible and filled with glory, obtaining the outcome of your faith, the salvation of your souls.* What is it about Christian joy that communicates who Jesus Christ is to a hopeless world?

5. How much does being too busy and agenda driven affect our joy? What are we missing out on when we consume ourselves with our own interests?

6. God must work in us before He can work through us. What does this mean to you?

I   *Interpret the Passage*

1. Looking at Philippians 2:12-30, identify key facts about the *who, what, where, when, why and how* of this passage.

2. Read Philippians 2:12-18 and answer the following questions:

   • What is Paul inviting us to receive?

   • What are we encouraged to sacrifice?

   • What are we exhorted to leave behind?

3. Philippians 2:12b (NASB) says to *work out your salvation with fear and trembling.* What does Paul mean? Why would believers need to do this?

4. Paul encourages us to *"shine like stars"* in a dark and depraved world. This was the same calling Jesus gave to His disciples in Matthew 5:14-16 (NKJV): *"You are the light of the world. A city that is set on a hill cannot be hidden. Nor do they light a lamp and put it under a basket, but on a lampstand, and it gives light to all who are in the house. Let your light so shine before men, that they may see your good works and glorify your Father in heaven."* Why are Christians called to let their light shine before the world?

- What extinguishes our light from the world?

- Who is responsible for our light?

5. According to Paul in 2:21, it is rare to find someone who has greater concern for the Lord's work than his or her own interests and schedules. What are Christians missing out on when they pursue their own agendas?

6. What things have you learned about Paul's source of exceedingly great and constant joy.

T Take This Passage into Your Life

1. Review Philippians 2:14-16. Is there an area in your life right now that you are grumbling about? Describe it. What steps can you take each day to improve your response to this situation? Who will benefit most from the changes you make?

2. Ask God to show you an area of your life He wants to work through so He can shine. Use your Journey Journal and write down what He reveals to you.

3. According to Philippians 2:12-16, how are Christians called to be in the world but not of the world?

   • Is there an area in your life you would like to be less like the world and more like Christ?

   • What are your greatest challenges to being Christ-like? What is tempting about retreating from the world?

4. Go back through Philippians 2:12-30 and put a star next to the verse or phrase where God is speaking directly to you. Write a prayer below asking Him to work in your heart, mind, and soul in the area(s) you marked. Be honest about your desires and fears.

5. Psalm 4:6b-7 (NLT) says, *Let your face smile on us, Lord. You have given me greater joy than those who have abundant harvests of grain and new wine.* Joy comes not from the material comforts of this world or praises of others but in knowing God and doing something worthwhile for His Kingdom. List the things you are doing to introduce people to Jesus and build His church.

God has not left us alone in our struggles. He helps us want to obey Him and then gives us His power to do His will. We just need to ask!

ℋ   Hear from God

1. How is God speaking to me through this passage?

2. What promises do I need to claim?

3. What are the things I can thank God for? Take time to thank Him.

4. What is God convicting me of that I need to change? Is there a sin to confess?

5. Who is God prompting me to pray for in response to this week's study?

6. What special truth did God teach me that I would like to share with others?

Journey Challenge

This week memorize Philippians 2:13

For it is God who works in you, both to will and to work for his good pleasure.

Lesson Five: *Joy in Believing* (Philippians 3)

𝓕   *Focus on the Passage*

Philippians Chapter 3 (ESV)

1 Finally, my brothers, rejoice in the Lord. To write the same things to you is no trouble to me and is safe for you.

2 Look out for the dogs, look out for the evildoers, look out for those who mutilate the flesh.

3 For we are the circumcision, who worship by the Spirit of God and glory in Christ Jesus and put no confidence in the flesh—

4 though I myself have reason for confidence in the flesh also. If anyone else thinks he has reason for confidence in the flesh, I have more:

5 circumcised on the eighth day, of the people of Israel, of the tribe of Benjamin, a Hebrew of Hebrews; as to the law, a Pharisee;

6 as to zeal, a persecutor of the church; as to righteousness under the law, blameless.

7 But whatever gain I had, I counted as loss for the sake of Christ.

8 Indeed, I count everything as loss because of the surpassing worth of knowing Christ Jesus my Lord. For his sake I have suffered the loss of all things and count them as rubbish, in order that I may gain Christ

1. Ask God to open your mind and heart to receive His truth and the Holy Spirit to be your guide.

2. Read the passage 2-3 times.

As you read, ask yourself...

3. What is going on in the passage (5 W's & H)?

4. What are the repeated words or contrasts?

5. What are the natural divisions in the passage?

6. What is the theme?

7. What questions do you have?

8. What word(s) bring you comfort?

9. What truth(s) are you having a hard time accepting?

10. What are you thankful for?

9 and be found in him, not having a righteousness of my own that comes from the law, but that which comes through faith in Christ, the righteousness from God that depends on faith—

10 that I may know him and the power of his resurrection, and may share his sufferings, becoming like him in his death,

11 that by any means possible I may attain the resurrection from the dead.

12 Not that I have already obtained this or am already perfect, but I press on to make it my own, because Christ Jesus has made me his own.

13 Brothers, I do not consider that I have made it my own. But one thing I do: forgetting what lies behind and straining forward to what lies ahead,

14 I press on toward the goal for the prize of the upward call of God in Christ Jesus.

15 Let those of us who are mature think this way, and if in anything you think otherwise, God will reveal that also to you.

16 Only let us hold true to what we have attained.

17 Brothers, join in imitating me, and keep your eyes on those who walk according to the example you have in us.

18 For many, of whom I have often told you and now tell you even with tears, walk as enemies of the cross of Christ.

19 Their end is destruction, their god is their belly, and they glory in their shame, with minds set on earthly things.

20 But our citizenship is in heaven, and from it we await a Savior, the Lord Jesus Christ,

21 who will transform our lowly body to be like his glorious body, by the power that enables him even to subject all things to himself.

A *Admit Where You Are*

1. Paul says in Philippians 3:8 (NIV), *I consider everything a loss because of the surpassing worth of knowing Christ Jesus my Lord.* List the people or things you have had to give up because of your relationship with Jesus.

2. Why are we tempted to put our confidence in our flesh (me-in-control) versus God (God-in-control)?

3. How might the things in our lives, which we have no control of, actually help us to grow in our dependence upon God?

4. What aspects of the Christian life feel like a race to you?

   - What do you think it means to strain towards the goal?

5. In what ways does your focus on the past prevent you from taking hold of what lies ahead for you?

6. In what ways are you enslaved to the things of this world? How do they steal your joy?

I   *Interpret the Passage*

1. Looking at Philippians 3, identify key facts about the *who, what, where, when, why and how* of this passage.

2. What is Paul warning against in Philippians 3:2?

3. What are Paul's credentials?

    *   What does Paul call his credentials?

4. Before Christ, Paul did everything by the book to try to earn his righteousness. How did that work for him? What was he lacking?

5. Paul wanted to know Christ personally and intimately, not just know about Him. What things did he want to share with Christ?

6. Paul compared his faith journey to a race. Look up the following passages and jot down things that give you insight on how we are called to train for this race.

    *   1 Corinthians 9:24-27

- 1 Timothy 4:7-10

- 2 Timothy 4:7-8

7. Summarize Paul's spiritual workout regimen.

8. What "training" exercises do you need to add or strengthen in your faith journey?

9. Paul says in 2 Timothy 4:7-8 (NIV), *I have fought the good fight, I have finished the race, I have kept the faith. Now there is in store for me the crown of righteousness, which the Lord, the righteous Judge, will award to me on that day – and not only to me, but also to all who have longed for his appearing.* Paul also tells us in 1 Corinthians 9:24-25 (ESV), *Do you not know that in a race all the runners run, but only one gets the prize? Run in such a way as to get the prize. Everyone who competes in the games goes into strict training. They do it to get a crown that will not last, but we do it to get a crown that will last forever.* Paul knew exactly where he was headed and he encourages us to walk with this same heavenly focus. Our citizenship is in heaven and we are sojourners passing through life with eternity in mind.

   - Is your mind set on things above or on earthly things? What can you do this week to change your focus?

   - The question for each of us is: "How well do I want to finish the race?" Write your answer below.

$\mathcal{T}$ Take This Passage into Your Life

1. What is the goal God has called you to pursue? What are some practical ways to keep your eyes focused on Jesus as you work towards accomplishing this goal?

2. 2 Timothy 2:2 (NIV) says, *And the things you have heard me say in the presence of many witnesses entrust to reliable people who will also be qualified to teach others.* Who is helping you train for the race? Is there someone in your life you can ask to be your spiritual mentor or trainer?

3. Titus 2:3-5 (NIV) says, *Likewise, teach the older women to be reverent in the way they live, not to be slanderers or addicted to much wine, but to teach what is good. Then they can urge the younger women to love their husbands and children, to be self-controlled and pure, to be busy at home, to be kind, and to be subject to their husbands, so that no one will malign the word of God.* Who has God put in your life that you can coach?

4. Jeremiah 29:11 (NIV) says, *"For I know the plans I have for you," declares the LORD, "plans to prosper you and not to harm you, plans to give you hope and a future."* Do you believe those difficult places in your faith journey are being used by God to prosper your faith? Why or why not?

    *   How can you grow in your ability to trust in God's unique work in your life?

5. Psalm 90:14 (ESV) says, *Satisfy us in the morning with your steadfast love, so that we may rejoice and be glad all our days.* Our human attempts to be good can be a barrier to our relationship with God. How do you spend time each day getting to know, enjoy, and follow the One who has made your relationship with Him possible? Do you need to make any changes?

6. 2 Corinthians 4:16-18 (ESV) says, *Therefore we do not lose heart. Though outwardly we are wasting away, yet inwardly we are being renewed day by day. For our light and momentary troubles are achieving for us an eternal glory that far outweighs them all. So we fix our eyes not on what is seen, but on what is unseen, since what is seen is temporary, but what is unseen is eternal.* Is there anything that is discouraging you this week and making you feel like giving up and quitting?

   • What truths do you need to be reminded of from your study in Philippians that will be an encouragement to you? Write them out.

May the God of hope fill you with all joy and peace as you trust in him, so that you may overflow with hope by the power of the Holy Spirit. Romans 15:13 (NIV)

ℋ   *Hear from God*

1. How is God speaking to me through this passage?

2. What promises do I need to claim?

3. What are the things I can thank God for? Take time to thank Him.

4. What is God convicting me of that I need to change? Is there a sin to confess?

5. Who is God prompting me to pray for in response to this week's study?

6. What special truth did God teach me that I would like to share with others?

Journey Challenge

This week memorize Philippians 3:13-14

Brothers, I do not consider that I have made it my own. But one thing I do: forgetting what lies behind and straining forward to what lies ahead, I press on toward the goal for the prize of the upward call of God in Christ Jesus.

Lesson Six: *Joy in Giving* (Philippians 4)

𝓕   *Focus on the Passage*

Philippians Chapter 4:1-20 (ESV)

1 Therefore, my brothers, whom I love and long for, my joy and crown, stand firm thus in the Lord, my beloved.

2 I entreat Euodia and I entreat Syntyche to agree in the Lord.

3 Yes, I ask you also, true companion, help these women, who have labored side by side with me in the gospel together with Clement and the rest of my fellow workers, whose names are in the book of life.

4 Rejoice in the Lord always; again I will say, rejoice.

5 Let your reasonableness be known to everyone. The Lord is at hand;

6 do not be anxious about anything, but in everything by prayer and supplication with thanksgiving let your requests be made known to God.

7 And the peace of God, which surpasses all understanding, will guard your hearts and your minds in Christ Jesus.

8 Finally, brothers, whatever is true, whatever is honorable, whatever is just, whatever is pure, whatever is lovely, whatever is commendable, if there is any excellence, if there is anything worthy of praise, think

1. Ask God to open your mind and heart to receive His truth and the Holy Spirit to be your guide.

2. Read the passage 2-3 times.

As you read, ask yourself...

3. What is going on in the passage (5 W's & H)?

4. What are the repeated words or contrasts?

5. What are the natural divisions in the passage?

6. What is the theme?

7. What questions do you have?

8. What word(s) bring you comfort?

9. What truth(s) are you having a hard time accepting?

10. What are you thankful for?

about these things.

9 What you have learned and received and heard and seen in me—practice these things, and the God of peace will be with you.

10 I rejoiced in the Lord greatly that now at length you have revived your concern for me. You were indeed concerned for me, but you had no opportunity.

11 Not that I am speaking of being in need, for I have learned in whatever situation I am to be content.

12 I know how to be brought low, and I know how to abound. In any and every circumstance, I have learned the secret of facing plenty and hunger, abundance and need.

13 I can do all things through him who strengthens me.

14 Yet it was kind of you to share my trouble.

15 And you Philippians yourselves know that in the beginning of the gospel, when I left Macedonia, no church entered into partnership with me in giving and receiving, except you only.

16 Even in Thessalonica you sent me help for my needs once and again.

17 Not that I seek the gift, but I seek the fruit that increases to your credit.

18 I have received full payment, and more. I am well supplied, having received from Epaphroditus the gifts you sent, a fragrant

offering, a sacrifice acceptable and pleasing to God.

19 And my God will supply every need of yours according to his riches in glory in Christ Jesus.

20 To our God and Father be glory forever and ever. Amen.

Philippians Chapter 4:21-23 (NASB)

21 Greet every saint in Christ Jesus. The brethren who are with me greet you.

22 All the saints greet you, especially those of Caesar's household.

23 The grace of the Lord Jesus Christ be with your spirit.

A   *Admit Where You Are*

Have you ever thought about the circumstances in your life where you didn't know the end result such as career decisions, finances, raising kids, health issues, family struggles, the state of our country, the state of the world? The unknowns in our lives often produce worry, anxiety, and sleepless nights. But God, with great patience and grace, shows us how much we let the unknowns rob us of the JOY He has for us today. God teaches us in His word that He is in control. He has it covered. He is working things out on the other side of our life's tapestry.

We do not know what tomorrow may bring, so we must choose to trust the One who sees everything and wants us to hear Him say each and every day:

> Trust Me. I will take care of you. I will prosper your faith. I will provide for you. I will protect you. I will put people in your life to encourage you. I will not give you anything you cannot handle. You may not see the end result but I do and I am pleased. My ways are better than your ways. Put your hope in Me and not in this world. I can do so much through you if you let go of trying to control and micro-manage your life. My power is made perfect in your weakness. I will equip you. You will not get lost if you continue to seek My Word for daily direction. It's not about seeing what tomorrow may look like. It's about experiencing the benefits and blessings of being with Me today.

Jesus tells us in Matthew 6:25-27 (NASB), *"For this reason I say to you, do not be worried about your life, as to what you will eat or what you will drink; nor for your body, as to what you will put on. Is not life more than food, and the body more than clothing? Look at the birds of the air, that they do not sow, nor reap nor gather into barns, and yet your heavenly Father feeds them. Are you not worth much more than they? And who of you by being worried can add a single hour to his life?"*

God is calling us to surrender our lives to Him and seek His best. This is not something we do once a week when we walk into church or attend a Bible study. It is the central, constant, reality in our life – a surrendered heart, attitude, and mind that trusts God with every aspect of our lives – the good, the bad, and the ugly.

1. What kinds of things do you worry about? Take time to examine your heart and write them all out.

2. What are the things you do to cope with worry? How's that working for you? Has worry ever accomplished anything good for you?

3. Are there any areas in your life that make you feel dissatisfied, fed-up, or resentful about such as your marriage, children, job, family, finances, body image or other area? How does having a discontented spirit manifest itself in your day-to-day life?

4. 1 Thessalonians 5:16-18 (NASB) says, *Rejoice always; pray without ceasing; in everything give thanks; for this is God's will for you in Christ Jesus.* What does this passage teach us about the way to achieve everlasting joy in all circumstances?

5. How do unreconciled relationships rob us of our joy?

   - Do you have any examples of this in your life right now?

   - What fears or concerns do you have about taking steps to mend those broken relationships?

6. What we put into our minds determines what comes out in our attitudes and actions. How are your attitudes and actions when you allow the things of this world to rule your mind versus the things of God? List any recent examples?

I   *Interpret the Passage*

1. Looking at Philippians 4, identify key facts about the *who, what, where, when, why, and how* of this passage.

2. Read Philippians 3:20-4:1. Why are we to *"stand firm in the Lord?"*

3. Paul warned the church of relational problems between believers. Read the following verses and list all the ways we can maintain unity among each other:

    - 1 Peter 3:8

    - Colossians 3:14

    - 2 Corinthians 13:11

    - Ephesians 4:1-6

    - Philippians 2:3

4. List the things Paul calls us to do in Philippians 4:4-7 when faced with difficulty?

5. Romans 12:2 (NIV) says, *Do not conform to the pattern of this world, but be transformed by the renewing of your mind. Then you will be able to test and approve what God's will is – his good, pleasing and perfect will.*

   - Read Philippians 4:8-9 and list the things we are told to practice that will help us renew our minds and experience God's peace each and every day?

   - List the things you learned about how to experience contentment from Paul's example and instruction in Philippians 4:10-19?

6. Romans 8:28 (NIV) says, *And we know that in all things God works for the good of those who love him, who have been called according to his purpose.* How does this verse help us to put our trust in God? Can you think of examples from the Bible where God turned difficulty and hopelessness into good for His glory? How about in your own life?

𝒯   *Take This Passage into Your Life*

1. Prayer opens our hearts to God so He can work in us and through us. When we cease praying, our hearts become cold, distant, and desensitized to God. Are there things in your life you are feeling anxious about and need to take to Him in prayer?

2. Jesus says to us in Matthew 11:28 (NIV), *"Come to me, all you who are weary and burdened, and I will give you rest."* Turn to you Journey Journal and surrender ALL your anxieties, fears, and worries to the Lord through a written prayer and allow Him to carry those burdens for you this week.

3. Paul says in Philippians 4:13 (NLT), *I can do everything through Christ, who gives me strength.* If we truly understand what it means to have Christ living in us, we would possess all the confidence and motivation needed to achieve any godly goal. What we often lack is an awareness of what we already possess in Christ. Take a few minutes and reflect on the power of God *in* you. What a contrast to the power of self. Spend time surrendering any attempts you are making this week to live on your own strength.

4. Do you see your trials and tribulations as places where God is training you to be content? What will you do this week to apply the lessons you learned from Paul on contentment in Philippians 4?

5. Take time to examine all that you pour into your mind. How much of it is *true, honorable, just, pure, lovely, commendable, excellent, and worthy of praise* (v8)?

- What are the things you should avoid?

- How will you do this?

- Ask someone to pray for you and keep you accountable to your spiritual health this week.

6. The church at Philippi provided Paul with financial support while he was in prison. However, it was not the gift, but the love and devotion from Paul's supporters that he appreciated most. When we give to those in need, there are mutual blessings between the giver and the receiver that result in joy. How about you? Are you finding joy in giving? If so, what is the reason? If not, what do you think is lacking in your attitude towards giving that is robbing you of the joy that comes from being generous?

7. Feelings of gratitude flow from a heart that shouts, *"This is the day that the Lord has made, let us rejoice and be glad in it"* (Psalm 118:24, ESV). What adjustments can you make in your attitude this week as God calls you to give?

Let us press on in our faith journey to get to a place where we can sincerely say, "Thy will, not mine, be done."

ℋ   *Hear from God*

1. How is God speaking to me through this passage?

2. What promises do I need to claim?

3. What are the things I can thank God for? Take time to thank Him.

4. What is God convicting me of that I need to change? Is there a sin to confess?

5. Who is God prompting me to pray for in response to this week's study?

6. What special truth did God teach me that I would like to share with others?

Journey Challenge

This week memorize Philippians 4:6-7

Do not be anxious about anything, but in everything by prayer and supplication with thanksgiving let your requests be made known to God. And the peace of God, which surpasses all understanding, will guard your hearts and your minds in Christ Jesus.

Bible Verses that Bring Comfort During Difficult Times

Psalms 147:3 – *He heals the broken heartened and binds up their wounds.*

Matthew 5:4 – *"Blessed are those that mourn, for they will be comforted."*

John 14:27 – *"Peace I leave with you; my peace I give you. I do not give to you as the world gives. Do not let your hearts be troubled and do not be afraid."*

John 14:18 – *"I will not leave you as orphans; I will come to you."*

Psalm 46:1 – *God is our refuge and strength, an ever-present help in trouble.*

Psalms 30:5 – *For his anger lasts only a moment, but his favor lasts a lifetime; weeping may stay for the night, but rejoicing comes in the morning.*

John 16:33 – *"I have told you these things, so that in me you may have peace. In this world you will have trouble. But take heart! I have overcome the world."*

Proverbs 3:5-6 – *Trust in the LORD with all your heart and lean not on your own understanding; in all your ways submit to him, and he will make your paths straight.*

2 Thessalonians 2:16-17 – *May our Lord Jesus Christ himself and God our Father, who loved us and by his grace gave us eternal encouragement and good hope, encourage your hearts and strengthen you in every good deed and word.*

Isaiah 49:13 – *Shout for joy, you heavens; rejoice, you earth; burst into song, you mountains! For the LORD comforts his people and will have compassion on his afflicted ones.*

Jeremiah 31:13 – *Then young women will dance and be glad, young men and old as well. I will turn their mourning into gladness; I will give them comfort and joy instead of sorrow.*

2 Corinthians 1:3-4 – *Praise be to the God and Father of our Lord Jesus Christ, the Father of compassion and the God of all comfort, who comforts us in all our troubles, so that we can comfort those in any trouble with the comfort we ourselves receive from God.*

Ecclesiastes 3:1-4 – *There is a time for everything, and a season for every activity under the heavens: a time to be born and a time to die, a time to plant and a time to uproot, a time to kill and a time to heal, a time to tear down and a time to build, a time to weep and a time to laugh, a time to mourn and a time to dance.*

Psalm 25:16-18 – *Turn to me and be gracious to me, for I am lonely and afflicted. Relieve the troubles of my heart and free me from my anguish. Look on my affliction and my distress and take away all my sins.*

Psalm 23:4 – *Even though I walk through the darkest valley, I will fear no evil, for you are with me; your rod and your staff they comfort me.*

John 14:1-2 – *"Do not let your hearts be troubled. You believe in God; believe also in me. My Father's house has many rooms; if that were not so, would I have told you that I am going there to prepare a place for you?"*

Exodus 3:7 – *The LORD said, "I have indeed seen the misery of my people in Egypt. I have heard them crying out because of their slave drivers, and I am concerned about their suffering."*

Psalms 22:24 – *For he has not despised or scorned the suffering of the afflicted one; he has not hidden his face from him but has listened to his cry for help.*

All Bible verses were taken from the NIV Bible translation.

Journey Journal

Lesson One: *Joy in Being an Encourager*

Gracious words are like a honeycomb, sweetness to the soul and health to the body. Proverbs 16:24 (ESV)

98

Journey Journal

Lesson Two: *Joy in Our Chains*

And the King will answer them, "Truly, I say to you, as you did it to one of the least of these my brothers, you did it to me." Matthew 25:40 (ESV)

Journey Journal

Lesson Three: *Joy in Serving*

Though you have not seen him, you love him. Though you do not now see him, you believe in him and rejoice with joy that is inexpressible and filled with glory, obtaining the outcome of your faith, the salvation of your souls. 1 Peter 1:8 (ESV)

Journey Journal

Lesson Four: *Joy in Obedience*

How blessed is the man who does not walk in the counsel of the wicked, nor stand in the path of sinners, nor sit in the seat of scoffers! But his delight is in the law of the LORD, and in His law he meditates day and night. Psalms 1:1-2 (NASB)

Journey Journal

Lesson Five: *Joy in Believing*

And do not forget to do good and to share with others, for with such sacrifices God is pleased.
Hebrews 3:16 (NIV)

Journey Journal

Lesson Six: *Joy in Giving*

Guide me in your truth and teach me, for you are God my Savior, and my hope is in you all day long.
Psalm 25:5 (NIV)

Bibliography

Bible Gateway: A Searchable Online Bible in over 100 Versions and 50 Languages. Web. Winter 2013. <http://www.biblegateway.com/>

Free NET Bible and Thousands of Bible Studies - Worlds Largest Bible Study Site. Web. 25 Jan. 2013. <http://bible.org/>

Hansel, Tim. 1998. *You Gotta Keep Dancin.* Colorado Springs: David C. Cook. Print.

Life Application Study Bible, NIV: Philippians. 2004. Grand Rapids: Zondervan. Print.

Precept Austin. *Bible Commentaries: Philippians.* Web. 25 Jan. 2013. <http://www.preceptaustin.org/>

Stedman, Ray C. 1997. *Adventuring through the Bible: A Comprehensive Guide to the Entire Bible. Christ Our Confidence and Our Strength, Philippians.* Grand Rapids: Discovery House. Print.

Stedman, Ray C. *Authentic Christianity: Bible Studies in the Book of Philippians.* Web. 25 Jan. 2013. <http://www.raystedman.org/>

Wangerin, Walter. 1992. *Mourning into Dancing.* Grand Rapids: Zondervan. Print.

Wiersbe, Warren W. 2007. *The Wiersbe Bible Study Series: Philippians.* Colorado Springs: David C. Cook. Print

Leader's Guide

Being a leader of a Faith Journey Bible Study is both a challenging and rewarding endeavor. By your willingness to lead other women in their journey with the Lord, you are allowing the Holy Spirit to direct you and use you for His glory. I know you will be blessed and it is my desire that you will grow tremendously in the Lord by taking on the role of leading your own study. Our goal as leaders should be first and foremost, to seek a closer relationship with God and encourage the women in our groups to make a stronger connection with Him also. It is so exciting to see His kingdom expand and women drawing closer to our Savior as they study His Word together.

Format...

Here is what I have found to be an effective format for leading a study:

1. Open each study session with a short prayer inviting God to be present and lead your discussion.

2. Review each section together...

   - *Focus on the Passage.* Read the passage aloud. It tends to work well going around the circle with each woman reading a few verses. This gives everyone an opportunity to be refreshed on what the Scripture says and also include those women who were not able to complete their study that week. Ask your group if they have any questions or if there are parts of the study they want to discuss in particular. Take this time to answer specific questions about the study. If you don't have an answer, or are not sure how to respond, don't be afraid to admit that you're baffled. Assign the topic as a research project for someone to report on the following week or tell them that you will do further research and let them know what you find out.

   - *Admit Where You Are.* This section gives everyone an opportunity to reflect on the passage and be introspective with some personal questions or thoughts to consider. You may want to take few minutes as you begin your study to ask a question or two of the group. If you have a large group, you may want to ask them to turn to the woman next to them and share one of the questions that they found meaningful that week.

- *Interpret the Passage.* This section asks questions that will encourage the women to go deeper into the passage to understand the context of what they are learning and pull out main points of the lesson. Ask your group to share what they learned when answering these questions. Don't put anyone on the spot. Allow the women to contribute, as they feel led. If no one offers to share, you can discuss something that was meaningful to you.

- *Take This Passage into Your Life.* This section is more personal and focuses on what is learned through the passage. Again, you may want to ask your group if they would like to share something that the Lord taught them through these questions. You might consider asking each question aloud and letting those who feel comfortable share.

- *Hear From God.* This section is very personal and some women may not want to share their thoughts here. Ask if someone would like to share with the group a specific thing they learned that week or something God is teaching them. This is also a good time to discuss the Journey Challenge and how your group experienced this activity.

3. In closing, ask for prayer requests and give your group the opportunity to pray for one another. I suggest that you use a few lines in the Journey Journal pages to write down the prayer requests so that everyone can continue praying for them throughout the week. If you have time, pray together for each request before closing your session. Some of the women in your group will feel comfortable praying aloud and others won't. I suggest having one woman open in prayer and another one close leaving some time open in between for anyone to pray if they feel led.

Tools for discussion and understanding Bible passages...

When leading a study, it is very important to have a good understanding of the text. The following resources are recommended to help you prepare for facilitating your group discussions:

1. **A Study Bible** that is filled with helpful footnotes, explanations and cross-references as well as maps, word lists, chronologies, and subject indexes.

2. **A Bible Dictionary** that will give you an introduction to every major word, person, or event in the Bible in alphabetical order.

3. **An English Dictionary** is helpful too for looking up words where the meaning is unclear.

4. **A Bible Concordance** that lists every word that appears in the Bible alphabetically and all the passages using that word, or a shortened or concise concordance that lists all the major words with the key references where they occur. These resources are very helpful in searching for other passages that relate to the theme of the study. For instance, if "faith" is a focus in the passage you are studying, you can look that up in the concordance to find out where it is used in other parts of Scripture.

5. **A Bible Handbook** will provide you with brief introductions to each book of the Bible and may also contain useful information about historical circumstances, archaeological findings, and customs of the people of the Bible.

6. **Commentaries** are useful for gaining perspective on a certain passage by reading what Bible scholars have gleaned from the passage especially when Scripture may be difficult to understand. They are not intended to replace the inspiration and authority of Scripture, and should only be used to enhance personal study.

Suggestions for successful discussion...

1. Good group Bible studies are interactive, not lectures. Much learning takes place when each member studies the Scriptures personally and has an opportunity to discuss and interact with other group members. This style of group facilitation will move your group from being passive to active and the Bible study becomes a life-changing experience for everyone. Be transparent as a leader, but be careful not to monopolize the time talking about your own experiences. It takes at least six seconds for the human brain to respond to a question, so wait a bit before jumping in with your own answers or responses. If you start answering first, your group will expect you to do this each week and will not share as easily.

2. Be sensitive to every member of your group. Listen attentively when they describe what they have learned. You may be surprised at their insights. Many questions do not have "right" answers, particularly questions that are aimed at meaning or application. These questions should lead you to explore the passage more thoroughly. Be affirming whenever you can. This will encourage the more hesitant women in your study to participate.

3. Stress confidentiality to your group. Create an environment where everyone feels comfortable sharing what is going on in her faith journey and to feel that they are in a safe place. You might want to say something like, "We want to have an environment where we can be transparent and share, and so our one rule is "whatever is shared here, stays here." This will encourage more open discussions.

4. The goal of group Bible studies is applying God's Word and deepening a relationship with Him, not just accumulating knowledge. The idea is not to settle every question or debate every issue Scripture may raise, but to respond in obedience to the central truth(s) of the passage. It is the leader's role to prevent the group from going off on tangents or trying to solve all the problems in the text. You don't want your group to leave without hearing and responding to the principle of truth, which is clearly stated.

5. Try to keep an eye on the clock and keep the discussion moving. If you've spent extra time on one question, it's okay to say, "Let's move on to the next section." It is not imperative to cover all of the material, but to be open to the leading of the Holy Spirit in your discussion. Be sure that you allow enough time for prayer and try to stick to your ending time to be considerate of everyone's schedules.

6. It is likely that some of the women in your group will not be able to make it to every study or they may not have had the time to work on their lesson. Encourage them to come to the meeting anyway and help them to feel welcomed. There is always learning and sharing that can take place even if homework was not completed.

7. Be in prayer for each of the women in your group between meetings and have a friend or two pray for you while you are leading your group. Prayer is powerful and the Lord will give you the wisdom and encouragement you need to fulfill your commitment to lead women in learning more about His Word and grow closer in their walk with Him.

About the Author

Lisa Thompson has been a Christ follower since she was 6 years old. She is passionate about reaching and encouraging women in all faith places to be transformed through an active and authentic study of God's Word. As founder of Faith Journey Bible Studies, her heart is to meet women where they are at, disciple them, and send them out to start their own Faith Journey groups.

Lisa wanted to bring the women in her neighborhood together to build authentic fellowship and study the Word of God. The women who came at Lisa's invitation were from many walks of faith or had no faith at all. Together, they went on a faith journey and God did amazing things in their lives. Out of that group, Faith Journey Bible Studies was begun. It has grown and continues to spread as more and more women use Lisa's Bible studies to start neighborhood groups of their own.

Lisa has written ten Faith Journey Bible studies with more to come. She also speaks at women's events and retreats, and is passionate about equipping leaders to go into the world and share the Good News of Jesus Christ with the disconnected and hopeless.

Lisa has been married to her husband Robb since 1992, they have four children, and call Folsom, California their home.

Made in the USA
Lexington, KY
15 July 2019